LITIGATION
ON BEHALF OF WOMEN
A Review for the Ford Foundation

by Margaret A. Berger

Contents

The Civil Rights Analogy   6
The Role of Foundations   7
Consequences of the Civil Rights Analogy   8

ECONOMIC DATA   9
In General   9
Changes in Women's Employment Pattern   10
   Nontraditional jobs   11
   The sex-segregated job   12
Recent Developments   13
   Fewer jobs   13
      Zero Economic Growth   13
      Proposition 13   14
      Deferred retirement   14
   Technological change   14

LITIGATIVE EFFORT   15
Constitutional Litigation   16
   Defeat of the initial strategy   16
      Rejection of strict scrutiny   16
      Disparate impact   18
   Gains achieved through the revised strategy of the WRP   18
      The successful cases   19
      The intermediate standard   20
      Stereotyping denounced   20
   Unsuccessful constitutional challenges   22
   Unanswered questions   24
      Protectionism   24
      Reverse discrimination   25
   Due process analysis   26
Employment Discrimination   26
   Title VII   27
      Facially discriminatory policies   28
         The bfoq defense   29
         The meaning of discrimination   30
         The pregnancy cases   30
         Pension plans   31
         Pay discrimination   32
         Sex harassment   33
      Disparate impact   34
         Future of Griggs   35
         Business necessity defense   35
      Disparate treatment   36
         Academic discrimination   36
         Hostility toward protesting workers   38

Problems of Title VII litigation   39
  The opposition has gotten its act together   39
  Title VII litigation is costly and getting costlier   39
  The use of class actions   41
Threatening clouds   41
  Finding an adequate class representative   41
  Restrictions on obtaining information   42
  Relief in Title VII actions   42
  The relationship between Title VII and affirmative action   43
Other employment-related activities by grantees   43
  Executive orders   43
  Job-training programs   44
  Military   44
Education   45
  Title IX   45
    Implementation by HEW   45
    Private right of action   46
  Vocational Education Act   46
  Constitutional challenges   46
Other Areas of Litigation   48
  Health   48
  Credit   48
  Property rights   48
Unlitigated or Underlitigated Areas   48
  Women as consumers   48
  Women and the criminal law   49
  Occupational and Safety Health Act   49
  Women and the family   49

EVALUATING THE LITIGATIVE EFFORT   50
Shortcomings   50
  The uncooperative attitudes of the courts   50
  The failure to reach certain groups   51
    Sex-segregated employees and blue-collar workers   51
    Minority women   51
  Drawbacks inherent in the litigative process   52
Importance of the Litigation Effort   52
  Litigation for implementation   52
    Governmental enforcement   52
    Enforcement by the private bar   53
  Litigation as a component of political action   54
  Litigation as a weapon   55
  Litigation and consciousness raising   55

MAKING THE LITIGATION EFFORT MORE EFFECTIVE   56
Improving the Case Selection Process   56
  Strategic concerns   57
    Identifying the appropriate approach   57
    Implementation   59
    Selecting the appropriate court   60

Grass roots organization   60
Case selection   61
Support for the litigant   61
Support for the litigation   62
Geographical organization   62
Alliances with other groups   63
Interdisciplinary input   64
Improving the Capacity to Litigate   64
The need for paralegal personnel and monitoring assistance   65
The need for a centralized back-up center   65

CONCLUSION   67

Appendixes   68
Persons interviewed   68
Questionnaire sent to grantees prior to interviews   70

Some Current Cases   71

This report seeks to answer two questions: (1) What has been the impact of litigation, and especially Ford Foundation-supported litigation, on the women's rights movement? (2) How effective is litigation as a tool in promoting equality for women? The analyses, conclusions, and recommendations that follow are based on interviews with the Ford grantees, as well as with other experts on women's rights (see Appendix A), an examination of judicial opinions, and some of the legal and social science literature concerned with women's rights.

At the beginning of 1979, it was evident that a deepening pessimism was prevalent among many of the active women's rights litigators. Some of them expressed strong feelings of frustration and bitterness about what they perceive to be the hostile attitude of the courts. Some feel that serious consideration should be given to abandoning the litigative effort before a truly catastrophic Supreme Court decision reveals to the public what these litigators believe to be true—that the women's rights movement, at least in the eyes of the federal judiciary, has not been wearing any clothes for quite some time. On the other hand, some of the more seasoned litigators feel that progress has been slow but sure, and about as fast as could realistically be expected for a movement with such far-reaching consequences. Interviewees outside the legal field generally expressed optimism, based on their perception of gradual, but steady, progress in the quest for sexual equality. They feel that lawyers take much too short-range a view, that they measure success in terms of the result in the case at hand, and that they fail to credit the indirect impact of their work. One litigator discounted these reassuring comments, explaining that the optimists are still looking at the wake left by the advocates' efforts, rather than at the leading edge of what is happening now.

This report begins by looking at the historical context in which the women's rights litigative effort evolved, and then analyzes the existing economic data to see if any objective changes have occurred. The report next focuses on key litigated issues to separate hopes from realities, and to determine whether there has been a pattern to the victories and defeats, and whether there has been an overall net gain or loss. Finally, some conclusions are offered on the litigators' achievements and an assessment on whether or not there is cause for disenchantment. Recommendations are then offered as to how litigation should be structured in the future in order to take advantage of the lessons of the past.

History of the Litigative Effort

THE CIVIL RIGHTS ANALOGY

While the roots of the women's rights movement extends into the nineteenth century, and the long and arduous suffrage fight culminating in the Nineteenth Amendment was over by 1920, the concerted effort to achieve equal rights for women through the use of the courts has a far more recent history. It was not until the 1960s that advocacy efforts on behalf of women began. That the effort was patterned on the civil rights movement is not surprising. A theoretical underpinning for such an approach had been suggested as far back as 1944 with the publication of Gunnar Myrdal's influential book, *An American Dilemma*, which drew a parallel between race and sex. As the women's rights movement grew, fueled by the works of De Beauvoir, Friedan, and Millet, legal literature built on the sex-race analogy emerged. Consequently, when it became apparent that despite the statutory changes of the 1960s, women were not going to achieve real gains unless these changes were enforced by the courts, the organizations and public interest law firms, which now became interested in litigating in the area of sex discrimination, saw the problem in the context of the then flourishing civil rights effort. They sought to emulate the movement's methodology, structure, and funding techniques. The test method, pioneered by the NAACP Legal Defense Fund, Inc., seemed equally appropriate for women's rights. As with civil rights cases, the cost factors, the desirability of developing the law consistently, and the absence of trained, specialized litigators in private practice, made litigation by organizations rather than by individuals essential. Since the funds needed for a major litigative effort far exceeded any monies available to these groups, they turned to the foundations for funding, and especially to the Ford Foundation, which had been a major source of support for the civil rights movement.

THE ROLE OF FOUNDATIONS

With the exception of the Ford Foundation, the response of the foundations has, for the most part, been disappointing. The then president of the National Organization of Women (NOW) Legal Defense and Education Fund concluded in a 1975 article that "[a]mong the giants, only the Ford Foundation has moved in all the appropriate ways to meet the needs of the feminists."[1] Less than one-fifth of 1 per cent of some 7 billion dollars of foundation monies disbursed between 1972 and 1974 has gone to support programs designed to improve the status of women[2]; at least one-half of this total has come from Ford.[3] A summary of 1976 grants to women's programs shows that the Ford Foundation has made over twice as many awards than any other foundation.

The Ford Foundation is currently funding four of the national membership organizations that are litigating sex discrimination cases: The American Civil Liberties Union Women's Rights Project; the NAACP Legal Defense Fund, Inc.[4]; the Mexican

1. Tully, Funding the Feminists, Foundation News 24, 25 (March–April 1975).

2. Ibid., p. 26.

3. Ibid.

4. This grant does not support litigation directly. The funds were used to support a program for minority women lawyers in the western United States through activities such as compiling lists of minority women attorneys, sponsoring workshops and seminars, disseminating information about litigation, and seeking assistance for litigation.

American Legal Defense and Education Fund (MALDEF) Chicana Rights Project; and the League of Women Voters. In addition, Ford is supporting three public interest law firms engaged in sex discrimination work: The Women's Law Fund of Cleveland, Ohio; the Center for Law and Social Policy—Women's Rights Project of Washington, D.C.; and Public Advocates, Inc., located in San Francisco, California.

CONSEQUENCES OF THE CIVIL RIGHTS ANALOGY

The assumed congruence between civil rights and women's rights did far more than shape the procedural approach of the litigators. It has caused them to measure their rate of success against that of the civil rights activists of the 1960s, and to view defeats in the civil rights arena as their own. Furthermore, since they see themselves as the heirs of the civil rights movement, they consider the bleak, early, discouraging years prior to *Brown v. Board of Education* as part of their own history, and they therefore tend to find irrelevant the Supreme Court's historical pattern of reaching a settled constitutional position on an issue only after years of litigation. As far as some of the women litigators are concerned, those years have already passed. Finally, and most importantly, as will be discussed in this report, the assumed parallel between race and sex has had a profound effect on how issues have been presented to the courts and on how support for these issues has been organized.

Reliance on the race analogy may also account for the singular inattention that has been paid to the implications of the women's rights movement. If one takes the litigative effort at face value, it purports to be concerned only with securing women equal access to jobs, schools, sports teams, credit, and other institutions of American life. But underneath the surface lie unasked and unresolved questions about the role of women in our society. It is not difficult to conceive of a society in which the color of a person's skin would be as irrelevant as the color of his or her eyes.[5] Eliminating racism would not require society to adopt new patterns of living. While the person next door, at work,

---

5. *See* Wasserstrom, *Racism, Sexism and Preferential Treatment: An Approach to the Topics,* 24 UCLA Law Review 581 (1977).

or at school might be of a different color from before, life in the home, on the job, or in the classroom would not be affected radically. But the elimination, or even partial eradication, of sexism would alter the entire fabric of our lives. Broad changes would have to occur in family life, responsibilities for child care, education, employment (Would we still have a 40-hour, 5-day work week?), welfare, and tax policy, to name just a few of the obvious areas in which change would take place.

By viewing sexism as analogous to racism and susceptible to correction by equal access, the implications of women becoming full and equal participants in our society have not had to be addressed. Blueprints for the future lie considerably beyond the scope of this study; however, the avoidance of these issues may account for at least some of the uneasiness the courts have displayed toward feminist issues, a distress attributable to their concern about these unarticulated consequences that might stem from their decisions.

Economic Data

IN GENERAL

There has been a tremendous increase in the number and percentage of women in the work force,[6] and in the total number of years that women are spending in the work force.[7] The number

6. In the period 1950 to July 1978, the number of women in the work force increased from 18 million to 42.1 million, a 129% increase (U.S. Dep'ts of Labor and Commerce, Sept. 1978). Women accounted for 60% of the total increase in the size of the work force between 1950 and 1976. In that period, the proportion of males declined from 86.8% to 78.1% as the female rate increased from 33.9% to 47.4% (Ginzberg, *The Job Problem*, 237 *Scientific American* 43, 45, 1977). In the period 1970 to 1975, the growth rate for the female work force was 13%, more than double the 5% growth for men (Improving Job Opportunities for Women, Conference Board Report No. 744, p. 17, 1978).

7. As of July 1978, the only age group in which fewer than 50% of women are in the work force is the group of women 55 years and older. 60.5% of women aged 25 to 54 years are working in 1978 as compared to 42.9% of the same age group in 1960. The increase has been most striking for women of childbearing years, e.g., from 46.1% to 69.1% for the 20- to 24-years age group, from 36% to 62.6% for the 25- to 34-years age group (U.S. Dep'ts of Labor and Commerce, Sept. 1978).

of married women in the work force is over five times as large as in 1940,[8] and in nearly six out of ten of all husband-wife families, both spouses hold paid jobs.[9] Despite these changes, the gap in earnings between male and female workers has increased over the past twenty years,[10] and the economic distance between rich and poor families with working wives appears to be widening.[11] This leaves the household headed by a woman (and we now have a 50 per cent divorce rate) at the bottom of the economic heap.[12] Minority women fare even worse; they suffer from a double handicap and earn wages considerably lower than those of other women.[13]

CHANGES IN WOMEN'S EMPLOYMENT PATTERN

Some change has taken place in the work force since the litigation effort on behalf of women began, but given the huge

8. In 1940, married women constituted only 30% or 4.2 million of all women workers. In March, 1978, 55.6% or nearly 23 million of all female workers were married. (U.S. Dep'ts of Labor and Commerce, Sept. 1978).

9. Over 58% of women with schoolage children are working; so are 41% of the mothers of children too young to attend school (*Wall Street Journal*, Aug. 28, 1978, p. 1, col. 1).

10. In 1977, full-time women workers had a median income of $8,814, while men averaged $15,070, i.e., women made 58.5 cents to every male dollar. In 1955, the female median income was $2,934 to men's $4,246, i.e., 64.3 cents to every male dollar (U.S. Dep'ts of Labor and Commerce, Sept., 1978). In 1976, a woman with a 4-year college degree could expect to earn as much as a man who had finished 8 years of elementary school.

11. "Labor force participation by wives whose husbands earn more than $30,000 jumped 38% between 1967 and 1974, while participation by wives whose husbands earned $2,000 to $6,000 increased only 11%"; article concludes that wives of well-earning husbands tend to get better paying jobs themselves thereby increasing income gap between rich and poor (*Wall Street Journal*, Sept. 8, 1978, p. 1, col. 1).

12. In 1973, when the poverty level for a family of four was $4,038, and a full-time female worker's average salary was $6,448 per year, it is not surprising that 20% of all households headed by women were below the poverty line: 54% of all working women head households. Women who are single, divorced, widowed, or separated from their husbands comprise 42% of the women in the work force; 67.6% of all women office workers are single, divorced, widowed or living separately from their husbands (United States Dep't of Labor, Employment Standards Bureau, Handbook on Women Workers, Bulletin No. 297, 1975). In 1976, the national unemployment rate for women (8.6%) was higher than for men (7%) (American Women Workers in a Full Employment Economy, A Compendium of Papers Submitted to the Subcommittee on Economic Growth and Stabilization of the Congressional Joint Committee, 1977).

13. While in 1977 white females had a median income of $8,870 (57.6% of white males), black females averaged $8,290 and Spanish origin females $7,599 or 53.9%, and 49.4% respectively of white male income. (U.S. Dep'ts of Labor and Commerce, Sept. 1978).

number of women working in sex-segregated jobs, and the slow rate of change vis-a-vis men even in those occupations where change is taking place, it is wholly unrealistic to expect women to be represented proportionately in the work force in the near future.

Nontraditional jobs

Despite the increased earnings gap, there are some indications that women are obtaining a greater share of some jobs traditionally held by men. It will not be possible to see exactly how much improvement there has been in the job opportunities provided for women even for the 1970 to 1975 period, until the figures from the 1980 Census become available. The Conference Board in a 1978 study concluded that real change was taking place in three areas of the corporate sector: management, professional and technical jobs, and craft jobs.[14] The *Wall Street Journal* reports that women now account for about 12 per cent of the nation's doctors, up from 6 per cent in 1950, and close to 10 per cent of its lawyers, up from 4 per cent in 1950.[15]

A look at some of these statistics indicates why employment parity, even in those areas where change is taking place, is a long way off. As to managers, the Conference Board found "that the rate of increase is considerably greater for women (+22 per cent between 1972 and 1975) than it is for men (+8 percent over the same time period)."[16] However, this percentage increase for women is large precisely because the actual number of female managers had been so small; the 22 per cent increase in women managers represents a numerical increase of 202,000 women, while the 8 per cent male gain means that a far greater actual number of men, 411,000, became managers. Little seems to be happening, because the greatly increased rate of change translates into a very small increase in the percentage of women managers. Women's percentage participation in managerial jobs rose from 15 per cent in 1972 to 17 per cent in 1975, i.e., a 22 per

14. Conference Board Report No. 744, see note 6.

15. *Wall Street Journal*, Aug. 28, 1978, p. 14, col. 3.

16. Conference Board Report No. 744, p. 10, see note 6.

cent increase in women managers amounted to only a 2 per cent increase in the proportion of women in the managerial category.[17]

Regarding the number of full-time scientists and engineers employed at universities and colleges, the National Science Foundation has reported that in a two-year period since 1974, women showed a relative gain in employment that was over two and one-half times that of men. Yet the proportion of total full-time female scientists and engineers rose by only one percentage point from 15 per cent to 16 per cent. It is still too early to tell whether this slow rate of change constitutes real change or tokenism at the bottom. For instance, women are barely visible at top management levels, and the woman who gets hired as an instructor or assistant professor has had difficulty in achieving tenure and/or promotion.[18]

The sex-segregated job

Very few women perform the same work as men.[19]

> The characteristic feature of our very large female labor force has been—and continues to be—severe occupational segregation. Unlike the men, most women workers are crowded into a relatively narrow range of lower paying, less desirable occupations. They are also heavily concentrated within certain industries that rely heavily on these occupations. Despite recent efforts to broaden the range of occupational roles available to women, "traditionally female" occupations still persist, and the overall employment profiles of women workers continue to be quite separate and distinct from those of males.

In 1950, 76 per cent of women worked as clerical and sales personnel, as operators in factories, or as service workers; in 1976, 73 per cent of working women were still so employed. Thus, at the

---

17. Ibid.

18. Of 1,182 chemistry professors at thirty-five major universities, only 34 are women; 8 of these women are tenured. In 1976, 12% of all chemistry Ph.D.'s were earned by women (*Wall Street Journal*, October 24, 1978, p. 1). Only 8.6% of all professors on full-time faculties were women in 1975 to 1976 even though women constituted 24.3% of the full-time faculties (WEAL Fund, Facts About Women in Higher Education 8, July 1977).

19. Conference Board Report No. 744, p. 10, see note 6.

end of the period as at the beginning, three out of four women were still concentrated in these occupations.[20]

If current job profiles continue, the typical female worker who is entering the job force in such great numbers will always work at a sex-segregated job, and will accordingly be paid poorly. History indicates that jobs held predominantly by women have never been recompensed at the same rate as jobs held by men.[21] The rate of pay for a job initially handled by men has always dropped when it was reassigned to women, as was the case with secretaries. Even identical jobs being performed contemporaneously command vastly different wages depending on whether they are classified as male or female. The Equal Opportunity Commission discovered that "framemen" working for the telephone company earned much less at Michigan Bell, where the job was performed by women than at any of the other telephone companies where the job was classified as male.[22] Pay is low not because of the inherent nature of the work, but because it is performed by women.

RECENT DEVELOPMENTS

A number of recent developments, singly or in combination, could affect women's participation in the work force.

Fewer jobs
Zero Economic Growth. Women were able to enter the work force in such great numbers because there has been a rapid rate of job expansion in the past twenty-five years. What, however, will happen if the economy ceases to grow or contracts? What kind of jobs will women workers entering the job market be able to get?

20. Ginzberg, *see note 6*, p. 49

21. Wertheimer, *We Were There—The Story of Working Women in America.* New York: Pantheon Books, 1977.

22. EEOC Prehearing Analysis and Summary of Evidence, A Unique Competence, A Study of Equal Employment Opportunity in the Bell System. In Babcock, Freedman, Norton, and Ross, *Sex Discrimination and the Law* 288, 293–294. Boston: Little Brown & Co., 1975.

Will men, because of a decrease in sex stereotyping, be willing to take traditionally female jobs if no other jobs are available? Will women then not only have problems in getting new jobs but also in retaining jobs that used to be theirs? Or has the concept of equal opportunity for women been firmly enough entrenched so that it can weather economic crises?

Proposition 13. An acceleration of the Proposition 13 movement that would result in eliminating jobs in state government would undoubtedly have a disproportionately harsh impact on women. This is a relatively new area of employment that women have been entering in accelerating numbers, and the traditional employer response is to fire first those who were hired last.

Deferred retirement. The increased attention to age discrimination, and Congress's action in changing the mandatory age of retirement from 65 to 70 may cause more men to remain in the work force than previously, thereby decreasing the job turnover rate and the creation of job vacancies to which women may aspire.

Technological change

A technological revolution in data processing is affecting women in a number of ways. A substantial number of white collar secretarial and bookkeeping jobs are being converted into blue collar jobs. These jobs afford the worker less personal contact with her boss and fellow employees, and less of a stake in the business of the employer. Women who enjoyed doing clerical work because of the element of personal interactions may now find themselves with increasingly bad assembly-line jobs devoid of this kind of satisfaction. Whether this new development will convince office workers to unionize, which they have for the most part resisted to date, remains to be seen. Such a movement could have a tremendous impact on the wage structure for women because the already large number and proportion of female clerical workers continues to climb.[23]

It has been suggested that increasing the participation of

23. Conference Board Report No. 744, pp. 25, 27, see note 6.

women in nontraditional jobs will cause accelerated technological change detrimental to the majority of women whose traditional jobs are peculiarly susceptible to this form of innovation.[24] This is one interpretation of what has happened to the job profile at the American Telephone and Telegraph Co. since it signed a consent decree in 1973 providing for rigorous goals and timetables for increasing the participation of women (and other minorities) in the higher levels of management and craft jobs. After three years of affirmative action at AT&T, there were far fewer women workers than before, because automation had reduced the need for operators, lower level clerical workers, and the women who had supervised these jobs at the lowest levels of management.[25]

Litigative Effort

To date, the advocacy efforts of Ford Foundation grantees have been concentrated in three main areas: the Constitution, employment discrimination, and education. Some effort has also been expended on health and credit issues. Virtually no litigative effort has as yet been directed to the Occupational and Safety Health Act (OSHA) (although there has been some discussion of what should be done), the criminal process, or family law, except as incidental to the constitutional activity. Almost all of the litigation has been brought in the federal courts or has involved federal agencies. To date, almost no litigation has been based on state constitutions or statutory provisions. None of the grantees has used Foundation funding for abortion issues.

24. Hacker, *Sex Stratification, Technology and Organizational Change: A Longitudinal Analysis of AT&T* (unpublished paper presented at American Sociological Association Annual Conference, San Francisco, Ca., Sept. 1978).

25. Ms. Hacker's analysis is borne out by what happened at The New York Telephone Co. after the consent decree. In 1971 there were 103,000 jobs, at the end of 1978 there were 76,000. The drop was due to technological changes which affected accounting jobs and eliminated the need for operators (Interview with Robert Young, Director of Urban Affairs, Sept. 22, 1978).

CONSTITUTIONAL LITIGATION

In 1974, the strategy with regard to constitutional issues looked something like this: (1) establish that sex is analogous to race for purposes of the equal protection clause of the Constitution; (2) use this finding to attack federal laws which on their face contained sexual distinctions; (3) move on to attack sex-neutral government programs that have a disparate impact on women.

At the beginning of 1979, it was apparent that (1) there is no room for women in the definition of equality adopted by the Supreme Court in the context of its opinions on racial discrimination; (2) there has been some progress in attacking facially discriminatory federal laws; (3) disparate impact is a dead issue.

More than any other group, the Women's Rights Project of the ACLU (WRP) has participated in cases before the Supreme Court challenging sex-based discrimination on constitutional grounds.[26] The Women's Law Fund of Cleveland has also brought some cases before the Court.[27]

Rejection of strict scrutiny. The first priority of the women's rights advocates was to establish that sex, like race, is a suspect classification. Had the Supreme Court extended the full protection of the equal protection clause to women, the need for an Equal Rights Amendment would not have been as pressing, because there would have been an authoritative commitment to equal rights for women as a basic norm of our society. Had the Court been willing to hold that gender classifications must be subjected to close judicial scrutiny, the burden of justifying sex classifications would have shifted to the state, and women would no longer have been required to show that the classification in question rested on no reasonable basis, as the Court had required in previous cases where sex discrimination was al-

26. Reed v. Reed, 404 U.S. 71 (1971); Frontiero v. Richardson, 411 U.S. 677 (1973); Kahn v. Shevin, 416 U.S.351 (1974); Edwards v. Healy, 421 U.S. 722 (1975) (heard together with Taylor v. Louisiana, 419 U.S. 522 (1975)); Weinberger v. Wiesenfeld, 420 U.S. 636 (1975); Turner v. Dep't of Employment Security, 423 U.S. 44 (1975); Craig v. Boren, 429 U.S. 190 (1976); Califano v. Goldfarb, 430 U.S. 199 (1977); Duren v. Missouri, 99 S.Ct. 664 (1979); Orr v. Orr, 99 S.Ct. 1102 (1979).

27. Cleveland Board of Education v. LaFleur, 414 U.S. 632 (1974); Califano v. Stevens, No. 78-449, appeal filed 9/15/78.

leged. A strict scrutiny test would have shifted all the burdens of proof to the State—the burden of showing the overwhelming public purpose of the classifications selected, the burden of showing that the classification was necessary, and the burden of showing that no less drastic alternatives for accomplishing that purpose were available. Instead of being presumptively valid, sex-based classifications would have become void. Reliance on traditional sexist stereotypes would no longer have sufficed because the facts necessary to sustain the law would have had to be demonstrated by the state.

In its initial case before the Supreme Court, *Reed* v. *Reed*,[28] the WRP scored a significant victory. While the Court did not adopt the strict scrutiny standard, a central concern of the WRP's brief,[29] it did for the first time invalidate a statute on the grounds of sex discrimination. Two years later, the goal of equating sex with race for the purposes of the equal protection clause seemed almost within grasp. In 1973, in *Frontiero* v. *Richardson*,[30] the Court came within one vote of holding that sex, like race, is a suspect classification triggering strict scrutiny. Since then, however, even those judges who viewed sex as akin to race in *Frontiero* have retreated from this position.[31]

The Court's rejection of the race-sex analogy has had tremendous repercussions, both symbolic and strategic. It signaled that the war on sex discrimination was not going to be a lighting blitz, but rather a long drawn-out struggle. The Burger Court was not going to do for women what the Warren Court had done for blacks, and the feminist movement was not going to be able to piggy-back on the civil rights movement to any great extent. It

28. 404 U.S. 71 (1971). State statute giving males a preference over females to letters of administration violated equal protection clause.

29. Reed v. Reed, Brief for appellant:
   [J]ust as the Equal Pay Act and Title VII have not ended discrimination against women even in the employment spheres to which they apply, sex-based discrimination will not disintegrate upon this Court's recognition that sex is a suspect classification. But without this recognition, the struggle for an end to sex-based discrimination will extend well beyond the current period in time, a period in which any functional justification for difference in treatment has ceased to exist.

30. 411 U.S. 677 (1973). Justice Brennan, speaking for a plurality consisting of Justices Douglas, White, and Marshall agreed that "classifications based upon sex... are inherently suspect."

31. See Weinberger v. Wiesenfeld, 420 U.S. 653.

also meant that the women's rights advocates had to abandon a sweeping frontal attack in favor of a step-by-step operation.

Disparate impact. It had been the hope of the women's rights advocates that after establishing sex as a suspect classification, they would turn to attacking statutory classifications, which seemingly neutral, had a disproportionately heavy negative impact on women. They expected to use the same analysis that had been developed in employment discrimination cases brought pursuant to Title VII of the Civil Rights Act of 1964, where the burden of showing a permissible purpose for the classification shifts to the defendant once disparate impact is shown. In *Washington v. Davis,*[32] a case involving racial discrimination, the Supreme Court called a halt to this approach by holding that discriminatory effect alone is not enough to show a constitutional violation—proof of actual discriminatory purpose or intent must be shown. The difficulty of making such a showing has led to the abandonment of strategic efforts aimed at attacking sex neutral statutes that have a discriminatory effect. The litigators would not now institute an action such as *Personnel Administrator of Massachusetts v. Feeney,*[33] brought by the Massachusetts ACLU prior to *Washington v. Davis,* which unsuccessfully challenged the Massachusetts system giving veterans who pass civil service examinations an absolute preference. Although the majority of the court conceded that "[t]he preference operates overwhelmingly to the advantage of males," seven members found no demonstration "that the law in any way reflects a purpose to discriminate on the basis of sex."[34]

Gains achieved through the revised strategy of the WRP

Once it became apparent that the Court would not extend the full protection of the equal protection clause to women, the WRP abandoned its efforts to establish sex as a suspect classification. Instead, it concentrated on chipping away at sexual stereotyping through cases that demonstrated the inequities that may result to

32. 426 U.S. 229 (1976).

33. 99 S.Ct. 2282 (1979).

34. Ibid., 2285, 2297.

males from an unthinking application of generalizations about the sexes. A line of good results would, it was hoped, ultimately lead the Court to adopt a standard favorable to women. To date, the new objectives of the WRP have met with some success, which are detailed immediately below. The response of the Court to other issues, however, recounted further on in this report, indicates a profound reluctance on the part of the majority to undertake the kind of doctrinal development that would support a restructuring of woman's role in our society.

The successful cases. Perhaps the most important aspects of the WRP's triumphs before the Supreme Court are (1) that issues raised, endorsed, and argued by women have prevailed in the Court, and (2) that the results have been hailed by the media as victories for women. When one looks at the actual holdings, the constant thread that runs through these "women's rights" cases is that most of the winners have been men, and that women have won only when it was not at the expense of a man. In *Weinberger v. Wiesenfeld*[35] and *Califano v. Goldfarb*,[36] men received money when the Court found it a denial of equal protection to make certain Social Security benefits available only to widows, but not to widowers. Although a woman did win in *Frontiero v. Richardson*,[37] a case holding it unconstitutional for a statute to provide automatic benefits to the wife of a serviceman without proof of her dependency, while withholding benefits from a servicewoman's husband unless he demonstrated dependence on his wife for more than one-half of his support, the actual result in *Frontiero* certainly benefited the husband as much as the wife, since it made more money available for the family. In *Craig v. Boren*,[38] the

---

35. 420 U.S. 636 (1975). The Social Security provision that was held unconstitutional on equal protection grounds allowed widows with minor children to receive monthly benefits based on their deceased husbands' contributions but denied similar allowances to widowers with minor children.

36. 430 U.S. 199 (1977). Widowers had to show actual dependency on spouses to obtain benefits that widows received automatically; a plurality of four found the law to discriminate against women, while Justice Stevens, concurring, found the law to discriminate against men.

37. 411 U.S. 677 (1973).

38. 429 U.S. 190 (1976). See also Stanton v. Stanton, 421 U.S. 7 (1975) (a non-WRP case). No statutory distinction may be drawn as to the age of majority between males and females for child support purposes.

Court invalidated a state statute prohibiting the sale of beer to males under twenty-one and to females under eighteen on the ground that it denied males aged eighteen to twenty-one the equal protection of the laws. While women have succeeded in securing the right to be treated like men, but perhaps not identically to men, for purposes of jury duty, this line of cases rests more on the Sixth Amendment right to a jury selected from a fair cross section of the community than on equal protection grounds.[39] In any event, the result is probably not displeasing to the majority of males, since it reduces the likelihood of their having to report for jury duty, a privilege of citizenship which is not always viewed as such. In *Orr v. Orr*,[40] the Court struck down the Alabama statutory scheme providing that husbands, but not wives, may be required to pay alimony.

The intermediate standard. Although the Supreme Court has refused to extend strict scrutiny to gender cases, the Court has not returned to the position which it had espoused prior to *Reed v. Reed*.[41] Instead, the Court has adopted a new intermediate level of scrutiny that is more favorable to women than the pre-*Reed* rational classification test, but less favorable than a strict scrutiny standard. This intermediate standard requires the state to show (1) that the classification by gender serves important, rather than merely rational governmental objectives such as administrative convenience, and (2) that the classification is related substantially to the achievement of those objectives.[42] The intermediate standard reflects a heightened awareness of feminist issues on the part of some members of the Court, since it acknowledges that sex classifications cannot automatically be rationalized.

Stereotyping denounced. The WRP's objective of selecting cases that would expose sexist assumptions has been realized to some

---

39. See Duren v. Missouri, 99 S.Ct. 664 (1979). Justice Rehnquist, dissenting, argued that the language of the majority had strong overtones of equal protection; the majority left open the possibility of a state's tailoring an exemption from jury duty for those members of the family responsible for child care.

40. 99 S.Ct. 1102 (1979).

41. See note 28.

42. Craig v. Boren, 429 U.S. 190, 197 (1976); Califano v. Goldfarb, 430 U.S. 199, 208 n. 8 (1977).

degree. At least some members of the Court have made statements recognizing the pernicious effect of role-typing by sex and have expressed a consciousness of women's changing role in the market place, and in public and social life. Some of the language in the Court's opinions is heartening. " '[R]omantic paternalism,' which in practical effect, put women not on a pedestal, but in a cage,"[43] has been denounced, and "archaic and overbroad generalizations,"[44] " 'old notions' of role typing,"[45] and "assumptions as to dependency"[46] have been deplored. Some of the justices have noticed that "no longer is the female destined solely for the home and the rearing of the family, and only the male for the marketplace and the world of ideas,"[47] and have condemned "statistically measured but loose-fitting generalities concerning...tendencies of aggregate groups."[48]

This language certainly represents a change in the Court's attitude toward women when measured against statements such as those made by Mr. Justice Frankfurter, as recently as 1948, in a decision upholding Michigan's right to restrict licenses for female bartenders to women who were either the wives or daughters of male owners of licensed liquor establishments:[49]

> Michigan could, beyond question, forbid all women from working behind a bar. This is so despite the vast changes in the social and legal position of women. The fact that women may now have achieved the virtues that men have long claimed as their prerogatives and now indulge in vices that men have long practiced, does not preclude the States from drawing a sharp line between the sexes, certainly, in such matters as the regulation of the liquor traffic...The Constitution does not require the legislature to reflect sociological insight, or shifting social standards, any more than it requires them to keep abreast of the latest scientific standards.

43. Frontiero v. Richardson, 411 U.S. 684.

44. Weinberger v. Wiesenfeld, 420 U.S. 643.

45. Craig v. Boren, 429 U.S. 198.

46. Weinberger v. Wiesenfeld, 420 U.S. 645.

47. Stanton v. Stanton, 421 U.S. 14–15.

48. Craig v. Boren, 429 U.S. 209.

49. Goesaert v. Cleary, 335 U.S. 464, 465–466 (1948), disapproved in Craig v. Boren, 429 U.S. 210, n. 23 (1976).

Unsuccessful constitutional challenges

Women have fared badly when a victory would not confer a corresponding benefit on a male and/or when the issues presented to the Court were unique to women. In *Vorchheimer v. School District of Philadelphia*,[50] where a female plaintiff sought entrance to an all-male academic high school claiming that the facilities at the girls' school were not equal, the Court in a four-to-four decision, without opinion, affirmed the finding of constitutionality which had been made below. Justice Rehnquist did not participate. On the basis of his expressed views in sex discrimination cases, it seems evident that a five-to-four decision upholding the constitutionality of two school systems would have resulted had he not been physically incapacitated. Because the Court was evenly divided, the case does not have precedential value.[51]

In *Geduldig v. Aiello*[52] and *General Electric Co. v. Gilbert*[53] (which although brought pursuant to Title VII was decided on a constitutional standard), the Court held that the exclusion of pregnancy and pregnancy-related disorders from a company's disability plan does not constitute a denial of equal protection even though all other absences caused by medical conditions are covered, including those voluntarily incurred, because no pregnant man is treated differently from any pregnant woman. Accordingly, said the majority, there is no classification on the basis of sex, merely a sex neutral economic decision by employers not to include pregnant persons, regardless of their sex, within the plan.[54]

Taken by themselves, *Vorchheimer* and *Geduldig* might indicate only the Court's reluctance to undertake a restructuring of our institutions in the absence of Congressional guidance. But *Gilbert* was brought pursuant to Title VII, enacted by Congress,

---

50. 430 U.S. 703 (1977).

51. Trans-World Airlines v. Hardison, 97 S.Ct. 2264, 2271 n. 8 (1977).

52. 417 U.S. 484 (1974).

53. 429 U.S. 125 (1976).

54. One commentator has aptly commented on the "Alice-in-Wonderland view of pregnancy as a sex neutral phenomenon." Karst, *The Supreme Court 1976 Term- Foreword: Equal Citizenship Under the Fourteenth Amendment*, 91 Harvard Law Review. 1, 54n. 304 (1977).

and the EEOC had issued guidelines requiring pregnancy disabilities to be included under any available health or insurance plan. The majority sought to explain why, in this instance, unlike others, the administrative interpretation by the agency charged by Congress with implementing Title VII should not be entitled to great deference.[55] The suspicion remains that a majority of the Court is unwilling to impose hefty financial burdens on the loser (though the Social Security cases were costly),[56] at least in those instances where men will not benefit. Or, to put it another way, the Court has refused to alter the status quo cost of doing business in order to further the objectives of the women's rights movement.

Viewed in conjunction with the Court's ambivalent response toward abortion,[57] its position on pregnancy also suggests the inability of the majority to work out a theoretical structure for dealing with problems unique to women, and an unwillingness to allow women to decide issues of importance for themselves. The Court's insensitivity to the impact childbearing has on the ability of women to participate fully in our society suggests a lack of progress on the part of the majority in replacing the outmoded stereotypes, derided by some members of the Court, with a new vision of women. Generalizations about dependency have been decried; however, an absence from work due to pregnancy has been equated with an unpaid vacation, the tab for which will have to be picked up either by a male or the welfare state. These decisions bode ill for the present Court's willingness to adopt a doctrinal posture that would support efforts to restructure a woman's traditional role and her relationship with groups and institutions in our society.

55. *See* further discussion of *Gilbert* on pp. 71-74.

56. In *Wiesenfeld*, the government claimed the cost could reach $20,000,000 annually; *Goldfarb* was estimated as costing a third of a billion dollars. See Cowan, *Women's Rights Through Litigation: An Examination of the American Civil Liberties Union Women's Rights Project, 1971-1976*, 8 Columbia Human Rights Law Review, 373, 395 (1976).

57. *See, e.g.,* Maher v. Roe, 97 S.Ct. 2376 (1977) and Poelker v. Doe, 97 S.Ct. 2391 (1977) which substantially limited Roe v. Wade., 410 U.S. 113 (1973) by holding that state and local governments are not constitutionally compelled either to pay for nontherapeutic abortions for indigents nor to provide elective abortion services in municipal hospitals, even if facilities for normal childbirth are provided.

Unanswered questions

Thus far, the Court has not developed a consistent, theoretical framework for dealing with the issues of protectionism and reverse discrimination. In light of the Court's response to date in the equal protection area, the resolution of these issues may place new obstacles in the way of eliminating sex-based classifications.

Protectionism. To what extent is the specter of protectionism still with us? In its latest Social Security case, *Califano v. Webster*,[58] the Court refused to declare unconstitutional a provision authorizing a female wage earner to exclude more lower earning years than a male wage earner in making a computation on which old age insurance benefits are based. The Court perceived a remedial purpose to compensate women for past discrimination. Since it examined the legislative history of the statutory provision in reaching this conclusion, the Court did not merely conclude, as it had in some previous cases,[59] that the statute may have been designed to favor women. Nevertheless, the line is very narrow between the judicial sanction of legislation that seeks to protect particular women against specified dangers and judicial paternalism toward women because they as a group need protection. The protectionist philosophy of the nineteenth century, which became embodied in numerous laws, preventing women from competing with men "for their own good" is now viewed by feminists as having created the climate of opinion that made sex discrimination acceptable. It is not yet clear when a benign purpose of compensating women for past discrimination will past muster as an important governmental interest under the intermediate standard of scrutiny. In *Wiesenfeld* and *Goldfarb*, the Court had rejected the government's argument that the statutes were constitutional because they were remedial. In *Orr v. Orr*,[60] in which the WRP as amicus curiae argued successfully that a state law which provides that only husbands, and not wives, may be

58. 430 U.S. 313 (1977).

59. Kahn v. Shevin, 416 U.S. 351 (1974) (property tax exemption to widow, but not to widower, upheld); Schlesinger v. Ballard, 419 U.S. 498 (1975). This upheld Navy Statute that discharged female officers for nonpromotion only after thirteen years while male officers were terminated as soon as they were twice passed over for a promotion.

60. 99 S.Ct. 1102 (1979).

required to pay alimony, violates the equal protection clause, the Court stated:[61]

> [E]ven statutes purportedly designed to compensate for and ameliorate the effects of past discrimination must be carefully tailored. Where, as here, the State's compensatory and ameliorative purposes are as well served by a gender neutral classification [placing alimony obligations on the spouse able to pay] as one that gender-classifies and therefore carries with it the baggage of sexual stereotypes, the State cannot be permitted to classify on the basis of sex.

Reverse discrimination. Intertwined with the question of protectionism is the issue of reverse discrimination. How far may a legislative or administrative body go at the expense of men in rectifying past discriminatory treatment of women? The Court's failure to include sex as a suspect classification, or to work out an alternative, theoretical structure for dealing with the demands for sexual equality may prove particularly pernicious when issues of reverse discrimination are raised in the context of sex rather than race.

Even though the Court in *United Steel Workers of America* v. *Weber*,[62] endorsed "race-conscious affirmative action plans" in order to compensate for proven past discrimination, in a Title VII context, women will not automatically profit from such a result, if the equal protection clause, because of its history, is viewed exclusively as a racial provision.

Furthermore, at least some members of the Court do not seem to feel that the past treatment of women would merit parallel remedial measures. Justice Powell's language in the *Bakke* case is particularly ominous:[63]

> Gender-based distinctions are less likely to create the analytical and practical problems present in the preferential programs premised on racial or ethnic criteria . . . Classwide questions as to the group suffering previous injury and groups which fairly can be burdened are relatively manageable for reviewing courts . . . The resolution of these same questions in the context of racial and ethnic preferences

61. Ibid., p. 1113.

62. 99 S.Ct. 2721 (1979).

63. Regents of the University of California v. Bakke, 98 S.Ct. 2733, 2755 (1978).

presents far more complex and intractable problems than gender-based classifications. More importantly, the perception of racial classifications as inherently odious stems from a lengthy and tragic history that gender-based classifications do not share. In sum the Court has never viewed such classifications as inherently suspect or as comparable to racial or ethnic classifications for the purpose of equal-protection analysis.

Due process analysis

The Women's Law Fund of Cleveland has stood virtually alone in sometimes using a due process, rather than an equal protection analysis, in raising constitutional objections to gender-based classfications. In *Cleveland Board of Education v. LaFleur*,[64] the Supreme Court struck down provisions of two school boards mandating maternity leaves commencing four and five months prior to childbirth, on the ground that these mandatory rules amounted to an irrebuttable presumption of the pregnant teacher's incapacity which violated the due process clause.[65] The irrebuttable presumption test has not received a very good press from legal commentators,[66] many of whom, however, were writing at a time when the Supreme Court seemed to be willing to interpret the equal protection clause flexibly and with vigor. Now that the Court has retreated with regard to sex-based discrimination, the time may be ripe to reconsider using a due process analysis that allows the court more leeway to balance the consequences of the challenged classification without having to commit itself to a drastic all or nothing course of action.

EMPLOYMENT DISCRIMINATION

One of the chief objectives when the litigation effort began was to begin implementing the various statutes and executive orders

---

64. 414 U.S. 632 (1974). See also Yellow Springs Exempted Village School District Board of Education v. Ohio High School Athletic Association, 443 F. Supp. 753 (S.D. Ohio 1978) (discussed on p. 66).

65. See also Turner v. Dept of Employment Security, 423 U.S. 44 (1975), a WRP case where the Court applied LaFleur to very similar facts in a per curiam opinion.

66. See note, *Sex Discrimination in High School Athletics*, 47 UMKC L. Rev. 109, 110–113 (1978). And see, Weinberger v. Salfi, 422 U.S. 749 (1975) (retreating from conclusive presumption analysis).

that prohibit discrimination in employment. An attack on the pervasive patterns of discrimination that sanction the undercompensation and underutilization of women, would, it was hoped, lead to improved economic and working conditions. In addition, litigation was seen as effective in exposing the stereotyped assumptions which underlie employment situations, causing those affected to rethink their attitudes and to initiate change in the nonworking world as well.

Several of the Ford grantees have devoted a substantial portion of their litigative capacity to employment discrimination cases. The Women's Rights Project of the ACLU, the Women's Law Fund of Cleveland and Public Advocates have relied heavily on Title VII (see below). Other grantees have relied on Title VII to a lesser degree, but have dealt with other aspects of employment discrimination.

To what extent has the goal of eliminating discrimination in the work force been achieved? The public's perception of women's successes, fueled by extensive media coverage of the exceptional policewoman or telephone repair-person, seems to exceed by far the reality of what has actually been accomplished. The battle of employment discrimination is far from won; much more still remains to be carried out. As the statistics on the earnings gap in this report indicate, changes which could be attributed to the antidiscrimination laws are barely, if at all, visible at this time.[67] Numerous practices persist that are detrimental to women but are not yet proven to be discrimination. Furthermore, some ominous recent developments portend increasing difficulty in litigating sex-based discrimination claims effectively. Nevertheless, some significant victories have been achieved.

Title VII

Most of the employment discrimination cases have been brought pursuant to Title VII of the Civil Rights Act of 1964. The principal antidiscriminatory provisions of the Act are found in Section 703(a) which forbids employers

   . . . (1) to fail or refuse to hire or to discharge any individual

---

67. One commentator has concluded that the earnings gap would have widened more but for the impact of Title VII. See Beller, *Title VII and the Male-Female Earnings Gap: An Economic Analysis*, 1 Harvard Women's Law Journal 157 (1958).

with respect to his compensation, terms, conditions, or privileges of employment, because of such individual's... sex...; or

(2) to limit, segregate, or classify his employees or applicants for employment in any way which would deprive or tend to deprive any individual of employment opportunities or otherwise adversely affect his status as an employee, because of such individual's... sex...

Section 703(e) recognizes the employer's right to hire on the basis of sex where "sex... is a bona fide occupational qualification [bfoq] reasonably necessary to the operation of the particular business or enterprise." This is the so-called bfoq exception.

Facially discriminatory policies. The initial litigative effort, which utilized Title VII to attack overtly discriminatory policies, met with considerable success. The courts responded favorably by (1) striking down state protective legislation, such as that limiting the number of hours a woman could work, restricting her employment to certain hours of the day, or prohibiting her from working at certain kinds of jobs; and (2) finding that explicitly discriminatory hiring, assignment, and promotion practices violated Title VII. The early successes, in what are now perceived to have been the easy cases, probably led to more compliance with Title VII than can be measured by the reported decisions, either because of voluntary action by employers who feared litigation, or through settlements prior to trial. Blatant facial disrimination, not exempted by any defense, has probably in large measure disappeared.

Nevertheless, because the vast majority of women still work at sex-segregated jobs, this compliance has not narrowed the earnings gap between males and females. Furthermore, these cases often had little value in setting precedents so that the same issue had to be litigated numerous times against employers who refused to comply. Thus, although the Women's Law Fund of Cleveland successfully challenged numerous discriminatory practices of the Cleveland and East Cleveland Police Departments,[68] a suit brought against the Philadelphia Police Depart-

68. The Fund brought 11 separate federal court actions, challenging every aspect of police work from recruitment and hiring through promotion, and succeeded in obtaining a consent decree after 5 years of litigation.

ment by a policewoman represented by the WRP is unresolved after five and a half years of litigation,[69] and there are as yet virtually no women on the Philadelphia police force. These cases do, however, attract wide publicity so that they are undoubtedly significant in eradicating stereotyped notions about jobs for women even when their legal impact is limited to the immediate parties.

THE BFOQ (bona fide occupational qualification) DEFENSE
The grantees have not handled the garden variety cases of facial discrimination, but have sought to concentrate, with some success, on actions such as those in which sophisticated bfoq defenses have been raised. The Women's Law Fund, in addition to its police cases, has successfully concluded an action allowing a woman to become a zookeeper,[70] and the WRP has reached favorable settlements on behalf of women who wished to become waitresses in first class restaurants in New York City that heretofore had hired only men.[71]

Although the lower courts and the EEOC had insisted on a narrow interpretation of the bfoq defense, i.e., recognizing sex as a bona fide occupational qualification only when it goes to the very essence of the job, or where it is necessary to protect privacy interests, this restrictive approach may have been struck a blow by the Supreme Court's decision in *Dothard* v. *Rawlinson*.[72] In *Dothard*, in which the WRP participated as amicus curiae, seven members of the Court held that the State of Alabama could rely on the bfoq defense to justify refusing to hire women as prison guards. According to the majority, the essence of the job is to maintain security, and women, at least under the circumstances of "violence and disorganization" prevalent in Alabama jails,

69. See the numerous orders in Brace v. O'Neil, 13 E.P.D. 483 (D.C. Pa. 1975), 13 E.P.D. 485 (D.C. Pa. 1976), 567 F.2d 237 (3rd Cir. 1977), 14 E.P.D. 7719 (D.C. Pa. 1977), 16 E.P.D. 8177 (3d Cir. 1978).

70. Leach v. Cleveland Zoological Society (N.D. Ohio, E.D.) (Settled in 1978 for $10,000: $8,600 in damages, $1,400 in attorneys' fees).

71. A class action was brought on behalf of female waitresses and buspersons against the Hotel and Restaurant Employees and Bartender's Union, Local No. 1, against Restaurant Associates (encompassing ten restaurants), Maxwell's Plum, The Four Seasons, La Caravelle, Lutece, 21 Club, La Cote Basque, Charley O's, Le Manoir, Sign of the Dove, and Sardi's.

72. 433 U.S. 321 (1977).

would be unable to do so, since "the employee's very woman-hood would...directly undermine her capacity" to perform.[73]

The majority, conceding that "[i]n the usual case, the argument that a particular job is too dangerous for women may appropriately be met by the rejoinder that it is the purpose of Title VII to allow the individual woman to make that choice for herself," affirmed the extreme narrowness of the bfoq defense.[74] The language of the majority is suspect, however, for its action belies its words; no empirical data was presented in *Dothard* relating either to women's ability to maintain security or to the inmates' reactions toward women guards.

It is at yet too early to tell whether *Dothard* will be restricted to cases where the danger is viewed as particularly egregious, or whether the lower courts will pick up on the paternalism implicit in the majority's decision and extend the bfoq defense to other situations posing hypothetical work hazards either to the woman or to those whom the woman is in a position to affect.

THE MEANING OF DISCRIMINATION

THE PREGNANCY CASES. In *Gilbert* v. *General Electric*,[75] the Court held that an employee income protection plan that covered all temporary disabilities except pregnancy did not discriminate on the basis of sex even though such voluntary surgery as vasectomies and hair transplants were covered. There was no discrimination since all pregnant persons were treated equally, and, consequently, Title VII was not violated. Subsequently, in *Nashville* v. *Satty*,[76] a case in which the WRP appeared as amicus curiae, the court found that pregnant women could not be denied their accumulated seniority. The Court drew a distinction between refusing to extend to pregnant women economic benefits in the form of income protection, and burdening pregnant women by stripping away their accumulated seniority rights.

73. Ibid., pp. 335, 336. Justice Marshall, dissenting, replied: "With all respect, this rationale perpetuates one of the most insidious of the old myths about women—that women, wittingly or not, are seductive sexual objects. The effect of the decision...is to punish women because their very presence might provoke sexual assaults. It is women who are made to pay the price in lost job opportunities... (p.345).

74. Ibid., p. 335.

75. 425 U.S. 125 (1976). (See also discussion on p. 29).

76. 434 U.S. 136 (1977).

Despite *Satty's* recognition that some disadvantageous treatment of pregnant employees may constitute discrimination, the case does little to blunt the pernicious impact of *Gilbert* which continues as a threat, even though its actual holding has now been set aside by legislation.[77] The benefits/burden distinction enunciated in *Satty,* without any guidelines as to which label would apply to any given policy, is indicative of the Court's inability to develop a theoretical structure for dealing with pregnancy. It reflects the Court's discomfort with the role that pregnancy plays in the lives of women, and continues the pretense that all women engage in the dual roles of wife and mother solely out of choice and not out of economic necessity.

The message that clearly emanates from *Gilbert* is that sex discrimination can be legally defended when it would be expensive to rectify. This poses a real danger that other fringe benefit plans will withstand challenge on the basis of the *Gilbert* approved method of permissive, selective risks. *Gilbert's* disregard of the EEOC regulations which the Court had previously characterized as entitled to great deference and which clearly mandated equal treatment of pregnancy-related disabilities[78] may foreshadow attention to other regulations, such as, for instance, those narrowing the bfoq exception, or those recently adopted that would permit reasonable affirmative action programs. A final ominous note is sounded in *Gilbert* by the Court's utilization of equal protection standards in deciding a Title VII action. Since the intermediate scrutiny standard adopted for claims of unconstitutional sex discrimination legitimizes some sex-based discrimination, an incorporation of those standards into Title VII would dilute the definition of discrimination that the lower courts had evolved.

PENSION PLANS. In *City of Los Angeles* v. *Manhart,*[79] the Supreme Court held that the practice of requiring a 15 per cent larger contribution from female employees than from males to an employee-operated pension plan constituted discrimination pursuant to Title VII even though the pay-outs were identical. The

---

77. See discussion on pp. 77–78.

78. Gilbert v. General Electric Co., 429 U.S. 125, pp. 155–156 (Justice Brennan, dissenting).

79. 435 U.S. 702 (1978).

Court reserved decision on whether "it would be unlawful for an employer to set aside equal retirement contributions for each employee and let each retiree purchase the largest benefit which his or her accumulated contributions could command in the open market."[80] This question of whether an equal pay-in, but unequal pay-out, violates Title VII is currently being litigated by the WRP in the case of *Peters* v. *Wayne State University*[81] which challenges the pension and annuity plans offered by the Teachers Insurance Annuity Association and College Retirement Equities Fund in effect at the university. In a similar case, *EEOC* v. *Colby*,[82] the First Circuit found it impossible to distinguish between the situation in *Manhart* and a plan requiring contributions from women equal to those of men, but where the woman would receive smaller monthly benefits. This issue will undoubtedly reach the Supreme Court and pose problems not encountered in *Manhart*. If an employer-sponsored annuity plan has to both pay-in and pay-out the same amount for equally situated men and women, then in order to continue the same level of subsidy that presently exists for male employees, the employer would have to increase contributions on account of female employees. We have seen elsewhere that the Supreme Court has not, to date, found discrimination when greatly increased expenses would inure to the benefit of women. In *Manhart*, the Court left itself considerable leeway with a caveat that Title VII was not "intended to revolutionize the insurance and pension industries."[83]

PAY DISCRIMINATION. The Equal Pay Act prohibits unequal pay for the same job; it has been held not to apply unless the actual functions performed are substantially equal. Consequently the Equal Pay Act cannot be used to remedy the low pay which prevails for traditional women's work,[84] since women are not performing substantially the same work as men, even though it may be of the same economic value to an employer. In *Christen-*

---

80. Ibid., pp. 717–718.

81. Trial has been concluded in Eastern District of Michigan, Southern Division.

82. 47 U.S.L.W. 2417 (1978).

83. City of Los Angeles v. Manhart, 435 U.S. 717.

84. See statistics in Part II.

sen v. *State of Iowa,*[85] the employer university had objectively evaluated all the jobs being performed by its employees and had then paid lower wages to its clerical workers, who were exclusively female, than to its plant employees who were predominately male, even though the employer found the jobs to be of the same value. The WRP argued that even if the Equal Pay Act does not apply, Title VII prohibits sex-based pay differences for work of comparable value. The Eighth Circuit rejected this claim, finding that Title VII wage discrimination claims are governed by the standards enunciated in the Equal Pay Act, and that setting disparate wage scales for jobs of admittedly equal value does not violate Title VII. Thus far no court has mandated equal pay for comparable work. Whether a federal judge would be willing to make such a finding in the absence of a clear congressional mandate is questionable. Consequently, no legal handle currently exists for redressing the low wages found in the sex-segregated jobs in which the majority of women work. Title VII has had no impact on these jobs except to make them eligible for males, who are not interested in the majority because of the unattractive pay.

SEX HARASSMENT. Though numerous studies and surveys documented sexual harassment as a serious problem for working women, the courts were at first hesitant to characterize such behavior as discrimination pursuant to Title VII. The first judges confronted with the sexual harassment problem had difficulty distinguishing sexual harassment from flirtation or normal social intercourse:[86]

> The attraction of males to females... is a natural sex phenomenon and it is probable that this attraction plays at least a subtle part in most personnel decisions.

By 1978, a workable judicial definition of sexual harassment has evolved:[87]

> ...when a supervisor, with the actual or constructive knowledge of the employer, makes sexual advances or demands toward a subordinate employee and conditions that em-

85. 563 F.2d 353 (8th Cir. 1977).

86. Miller v. Bank of America, 418 F.Supp. 233, 236 (D.C., Ca. 1976)).

87. Tomkins v. Public Service Electric and Gas Co., 560 F.2d 1044, 1048 (3d Cir. 1977).

ployee's job status—evaluation, continued employment, promotion, or other aspects of career development—on a favorable response to those advances or demands, and the employer does not take prompt and appropriate remedial action after acquiring such knowledge . . .

However, numerous procedural and evidentiary hurdles persist. Just because a claimant may now be able to withstand a motion to dismiss does not mean that she will be able to prevail. To date, there has yet to be a single trial on the merits of a sexual harassment claim. Nevertheless, the courts' abandonment of out-of-hand dismissals is some indication that they are beginning to perceive the reality of the problem. An awareness that women are, but must not be treated as, sexual objects in the workplace is a necessary first step in restructuring working conditions between men and women. Judicial recognition of the prevalence of this problem may cause the public to achieve greater insight into its attitudes toward working women.

Disparate impact. In 1971, the Supreme Court held in *Griggs* v. *Duke Power Co.*,[88] a racial discrimination case, that facially neutral employment policies that disparately affect a protected class constitute discrimination pursuant to Title VII. The absence of intent to discriminate is irrelevant: "good intent or absence of discriminatory intent does not redeem employment procedures or testing mechanisms that operate as 'built-in headwinds' for minority groups and are unrelated to job capacity."[89] *Griggs* was viewed with delight by women litigators because it promised to simplify problems of proof, and to authorize attack on numerous company practices that had been impeding the progress of women in employment, such as height and weight limitations, requirements of previous work experience which women could not satisfy because of prior discrimination, union referral systems, prohibitions against interdepartmental transfers, and refusals to hire persons with illegitimate children. Furthermore, it was expected that disparate impact analysis would become even more important as employers abandoned blatantly discriminatory policies in favor of subtle forms of discrimination.

88. 401 U.S. 424 (1971).

89. Ibid, p. 432.

FUTURE OF GRIGGS

Despite *Griggs*, the difficulties of making out a case on a disparate impact theory are increasing as the discussion below indicates. Furthermore, ever since *Washington* v. *Davis*,[90] which eliminated disparate impact analysis in cases arising under the equal protection clause, the litigators have feared the same result in Title VII. Thus far, the five-to-four majority in *Griggs* has held, and the holding in *Griggs* has been reaffirmed in *Dothard* v. *Rawlinson*.[91] Nevertheless, some of the litigators are very pessimistic about the viability of disparate impact. The Supreme Court has already carved out a large exception by exempting seniority systems that perpetuate the effects of past discrimination from attack under Title VII.[92]

BUSINESS NECESSITY DEFENSE

Once it is shown by the plaintiff that a facially neutral policy is discriminatory in effect, the employer must prove that the challenged requirement is job related. The plaintiff may then rebut this proof by showing that other devices without a similar discriminatory effect would also serve the employer's legitimate interests. In *Dothard* v. *Rawlinson*, a bare majority of the Supreme Court held that statutory height and weight requirements for the occupation of prison guard were not job related where correlation had not been shown between these requirements and strength, assuming strength was a valid requirement for the job of a prison guard. Three concurring justices found that the appearance of strength rather than strength itself could be a valid job requirement, but joined in the result because the state had failed to make this argument. The concurring opinion reflects stereotyped thinking about women. It is difficult to conceive of the concurring judges approving of height and weight requirements on an appearance of strength theory had the job applicants been male members of ethnic groups which are smaller than the national norm, such as Asians or Puerto Ricans. It seems to be femaleness which is bothering them.

---

90. 426 U.S. 229 (1976) (see note 31).

91. 433 U.S. 321, 329.

92. International Brotherhood of Teamsters v. United States, 97 S.Ct. 1843 (1977); United Air Lines, Inc. v. Evans, 97 S.Ct. 1885 (1977).

The majority opinion recognizes the validity of height and weight limitations, and other restrictions as well, if they can be related to the job. The business necessity defense has been applied, *inter alia*, to would-be women police officers,[93] firefighters, and pilots.[94] There are some indications that employers are becoming more sophisticated in devising tests which can be justified as job related. The telephone company, for instance, is working on a test for climbing skills that would certainly impact disproportionately on women, since one of the major components is pulling strength. The company claims that such a test is essential because too high a percentage of their women employees suffer telephone pole climbing accidents.

Disparate treatment. Women have fared least well when they claimed that they were treated less favorably than others because of sex, although no specific discriminatory policies can be identified. In these cases, in which the proof of discrimination derives from statistical demonstrations of a gross disparity between women and men, the litigators feel that many federal judges are not applying the standards that prevail in Title VII racial discrimination cases. They sense that many judges do not respond to claims of sex discrimination with the same feeling of urgency with which they react to racial discrimination. This difference in judicial attitude is illustrated by the higher education cases, in which the courts refuse to acknowledge that women are treated differently, and by the courts' hostile reactions to the protesting female worker.

ACADEMIC DISCRIMINATION

Virtually every claim brought against a university or college for sex discrimination in hiring or promotion has been unsuccessful.[95] Yet studies that have examined the enormous discrepancies

93. *See*, e.g., Smith v. Troyan, 520 F.2d 492 (6th Cir. 1975), *cert. denied*, 426 U.S. 934 (1976). A Woman's Law Fund case; circuit court reversed successful result below and held that height and weight limitations were valid.

94. See Boyd v. Ozark Air Lines, 419 F.Supp. 1061 (D. Mo. 1976). The court lowered height requirement from five feet seven inches to five feet five inches.

95. Vladeck & Young, *Sex Discrimination in Higher Education: It's Not Academic*, 4 Women's Rights Law Reporter, 59 (1978).

96. In 1971–1972, women full professors made an average of $1,700 less than their male

between male and female academicians' salaries[96] and the much smaller percentage of women than men who attain promotion or tenure[97] uniformly characterize institutions of higher learning as bastions of sex bias. The legislative history indicates Congress's awareness of this state of affairs when it amended Title VII in 1972 to cover educational institutions by eliminating the exemption previously enjoyed by colleges and universities. Nevertheless, the courts have been willing to defer to academic decision makers, without undertaking an independent scrutiny to see whether the reasons asserted for rejecting or passing over women are pretextual.

One of the few encouraging signs in the academic sphere had been the First Circuit's 1978 opinion in *Sweeney* v. *Board of Trustees of Keene State College.*[98] The court voiced "misgivings over one theme recurrent in those [prior] opinions [challenging sex discrimination in academia]: the notion that courts should keep 'hands off' the salary, promotion, and hiring decisions of colleges and universities," and cautioned "against permitting judicial deference to result in judicial abdication of a responsibility entrusted to the courts by Congress."[99] Unfortunately, the Supreme Court vacated and remanded *Keene State*[100] because a majority found that the First Circuit had erred in imposing too heavy a burden on the employer to come forward with an explanation of its failure to promote plaintiff after the plaintiff had made out a prima facie case of discrimination. The majority's action, strongly protested by four dissenting judges, bodes ill not only for the higher education discrimination cases, but for all one-on-one cases in which the plaintiff is protesting discrimination aimed only at her rather than at a class. According to the majority, the employer need only "articulate some legitimate, nondiscriminatory reason" for its actions, a standard which the majority views as imposing a distinctly lesser burden on the

counterparts; in 1976–1977 that gap had widened to $2,316. Facts About Women in Higher Education, WEAL Fund 8 (July 1977).

97. While in 1975–1976 women constituted 41.4% of lecturers, 40.6% of instructors and 28.8% of assistant professors, only 9.6% had attained the rank of professor. Ibid, p. 8.

98. 569 F.2d 169 (1st Cir. 1978).

99. Ibid., p. 176.

100. 99 S.Ct. 295 (1978).

employer than having to establish or prove a nondiscriminatory motive (the standard applied by the lower court). Since the problem in academic cases has always been the lack of objective criteria for evaluating a teacher's classroom work, research, and publications[101]—the usual indices for educational advancement—the decision in *Keene State* invites the employer to rely on subjective determinations without having to explain that sex bias did not enter into the woman's failure. The grantees had been shying away from academic employment cases, while conceding their great importance, even before this latest pronouncement by the Supreme Court.

HOSTILITY TOWARD PROTESTING WORKERS

The language in numerous opinions testifies to the repugnance with which some judges have viewed women who aggressively protest discriminatory treatment. The woman plaintiff has been characterized as pushy,[102] oversensitive,[103] a troublemaker,[104] and has been ridiculed as viewing herself "as a modern Jeanne d'Arc,"[105] to give but a few examples. Two law professors concluded on the basis of a study that:[106]

> ...by and large, the performance of American judges in the area of sex discrimination can be succinctly described as ranging from poor to abominable. With some notable exceptions, they have failed to bring to sex discrimination cases those judicial values of detachment, reflection, and critical analysis that have served them so well with respect to other sensitive issues.

While the quotation above was written in 1971, litigators in 1978 were still expressing the same assessment.[107] The majority's

---

101. One interesting, direct side effect of the academic litigation effort has been the development of a method for measuring objectively the work of a scientist through a system of citation analysis. See Geller, DeCani & Davies, *Lifetime Citation Rates to Compare Scientists' Work*, 236 Social Science Research 1 (1978); Aaronson, *The Footnotes of Science*, Mosaic (March-April 1975).

102. Fogg v. New England Telephone & Telegraph Co., 5 E.P.D. §8010 (D.N.H. 1972).

103. Thomas v. J.C. Penney, 9 E.P.D. 10,130 (D. Tex. 1975).

104. Johnson v. University of Pittsburgh, 359 F. Supp. 1002 (W.D. Pa. 1973).

105. Faro v. New York University, 502 F.2d 1229, 1231 (2d Cir. 1974).

106. Johnston & Knapp, *Sex Discrimination by Law: A Study in Judicial Perspective*, 46 NYU Law Review 675, 676 (1971).

107. See also Dunlap, *The Legal Road to Equal Employment Opportunity*, American Woman Workers In a Full Employment Economy, A Compendium of Papers Submitted

opinion in *Keene State* will undoubtedly intensify the employer's tendency to characterize the protesting female worker as a troublemaker who did not know her place and got what she deserved. Judging from the past attitude of the courts, the results may well be a failure to find discrimination.

Problems of Title VII litigation. Litigators are now confronted by numerous obstacles in Title VII actions, in part as a consequence of the substantive developments detailed above.

THE OPPOSITION HAS GOTTEN ITS ACT TOGETHER
Everyone is agreed that the days of easy victories with voluntary settlements culminating in consent decrees are just about over. Now that the cases are beginning to threaten the continued existence of established economic relationships which exclude women, the opposition has geared up, is digging in its heels, and is fighting every step of the way, while conceding nothing. Employers realize that the subtler forms of discrimination presently being challenged are expensive to prove; they are putting plaintiffs to the proof, and are, in addition, raising bfoq and business necessity defenses which are costly to refute.

TITLE VII LITIGATION IS COSTLY AND GETTING COSTLIER
Unlike the constitutional cases, which raise primarily issues of law and are relatively inexpensive to litigate, Title VII cases, for the most part, turn on disputed issues of fact, i.e., how the employer treated the complaining employee or group of employees as compared to other employees. Consequently, Title VII cases are becoming ever more difficult to litigate because of the cost of discovery and the need for expensive experts. The Supreme Court is increasingly stressing the need to establish disparate impact and disparate treatment by statistical evidence.[108] As record keeping has become more sophisticated, the amount of information that a court requires a plaintiff to consider for the purposes of statistical analysis has burgeoned. Access to

to the Subcommittee on Economic Growth and Stabilization of the Joint Economic Committee Congress of the United States, 95th Cong., 1st Sess. 61, 69-70 (1977). (Author concludes that the courts apply a different standard to the worker protesting racial discrimination.)

108. See, e.g., Hazelwood, School District v. United States, 97 S.Ct. 2736 (1977) and International Brotherhood of Teamsters v. United States, 97 S.Ct. 1843 (1977).

a computer is a must and statisticians are essential: initially to guide the plaintiffs in gathering the requisite information, and subsequently to testify in court as experts to explain the significance of the data. In the pregnancy cases, extensive medical evidence was introduced by the plaintiffs on the lack of ill effects due to working while pregnant. The cost of combating the bfoq and business necessity defenses has increased as well. Expert testimony may be required in order to refute the studies and statistics offered by the defense.

The growing difficulties in proof mean that a Title VII action cannot be won unless the plaintiff undertakes extensive discovery.[109] Aside from being initially expensive and time-consuming, the discovery process affords a determined opponent numerous opportunities to escalate the cost of the proceedings even more. Provided defendants are willing to spend money to combat Title VII claims, and there is every indication of an increased willingness on their part to do so, they can launch an all out paper war, expanding the scope of discovery through their own demands for information, while resisting plaintiffs' requests. Plaintiffs are forced into further expenditures of time and money if they want to move the action along. While the enormous cost of discovery is not unique to Title VII actions, the pervasiveness of the problem has prompted cries for reform.[110] The harm is particularly acute when, as in Title VII actions, there is an enormous disparity between the financial resources of the parties.

The cost of trial has increased correspondingly. Because of the vast amount of proof now considered relevant and its complex nature, requiring expert testimony as a matter of course, both the time for preparation and the time of actual trial are lengthening. Avoidance of these problems by entering at the appellate level is risky because if an adequate record is not developed at trial, appellate counsel may be precluded from raising certain issues on appeal. The availability of attorneys' fees and costs upon success does not solve the problem of funding a litigative effort that may extend over a period of years.

109. The magnitude is suggested by the report of an unsuccessful plaintiff in an individual action that she donated 1,000 pounds of court papers to a research library.

110. See Segal, *Survey of Literature on Discovery From 1970 to the Present: Expressed Dissatisfactions and Proposed Reform*, Federal Judicial Center (1978).

THE USE OF CLASS ACTIONS

The foregoing problems are particularly acute when an action is brought not on an individual basis but on behalf of an entire group of women similarly situated. A class action is clearly preferable for numerous reasons: It gives the plaintiffs more clout in obtaining a settlement, it is easier to counter an employer's justifications for unequal treatment when an entire class has been affected, and class relief is much more effective in overcoming discrimination than individual relief. Nevertheless, the astronomical increase in the cost and complexity of a Title VII action when it is brought on behalf of a group has led some of the grantees to conclude that they cannot afford to handle Title VII class action litigation. Even those who are willing do not have the personnel or monetary resources to handle the really big case. Since the EEOC has, in the last few years, been ignoring the instances of systemic discrimination, this had led to a situation where the greater the discrimination, the less likely it is that anyone is going to be able to attack it has been created.

Threatening clouds. Litigators are also concerned with a number of recent developments which they fear could have adverse effects on women's rights litigation.

FINDING AN ADEQUATE CLASS REPRESENTATIVE

Since the named plaintiff in class action suits takes the brunt of employer retaliation and judicial scapegoating, it has never been easy to find willing plaintiffs. Now the Supreme Court has suggested greater scrutiny by the lower courts to determine whether the class representative truly possesses the same interests, and has suffered the same injuries, as members of the class.[111] The danger exists that the Court's statement will be interpreted as barring class action certification unless an exact match is found between the proposed representative and the class. In one recent case, a district court judge found that an "activist" could not discharge her fiduciary obligation to a class because she might be affected by her own political interests rather than the interests of the class.[112]

111. East Texas Motor Freight Stystem, Inc. v. Rodriguez, 97 S.Ct. 1891 (1977).

112. Rossini v. Ogilvy & Mather, 77-1713 C.L.B., New York Law Journal, Oct. 20 1978, p. 1, col. 4.

Restrictions on obtaining information

One way in which the cost of litigation could be lessened would be by giving the litigators access to information which the EEOC has obtained under its investigatory powers. If the litigators could obtain this material prior to suit, it would simplify and reduce the cost of investigations. Two circuits have now ruled, one in the context of an action brought by the Women's Law Fund,[113] that investigative materials contained in the files of the EEOC may not be released even to charging parties, because this would have the effect of "fueling private lawsuits" and might interfere with the EEOC's conciliation procedures, which were viewed by one court as the primary mechanism to achieve Title VII's objectives. A related problem in which the Center on Law and Social Policy has been actively involved concerns efforts by women's groups via the Freedom of Information Act to obtain data on employment practices contained in affirmative action plans which federal contractors must file with the EEOC. This information would be useful, not only for litigation, but also for educating the public about the existence and extent of discrimination. Thus far, the Supreme Court has refused to decide this issue on which lower courts have differed.

Relief in Title VII actions

A study has shown that class relief benefiting the group of workers against whom discrimination has been shown has rarely been awarded in Title VII actions, and even less frequently in sex than race discrimination cases.[114] Furthermore, the Supreme Court in *Teamsters v. United States*,[115] denied the granting of relief to any member of the class who had not actually applied for a better paying job unless the nonapplicant could prove that he would have applied for the job but for the discriminatory practices. Compensatory relief, which the Women's Law Fund had convinced the district court to grant in *Harrington v. Van-*

---

113. *See* Sears Roebuck & Co. v. EEOC, 581 F.2d 941 (D.C. Cir. 1978) and see Burlington Northern Inc. v. EEOC, 582 F.2d 1097 (7th Cir. 1978).

114. Dunlap (see note 101), pp. 62–63. Reported cases for the years 1965 through mid-1975 "indicate that in only 13 per cent of all sex discrimination cases have courts ordered any class relief, to wit, injunctions benefitting groups of workers, back pay awards to groups, and related remedies"; the comparable rate in race cases was 24 per cent.

115. 97 S.Ct. 1843 (1977).

dalia-Butler Board of Education[116] to a teacher who had been assigned to an inferior teaching facility on account of her sex, was held on appeal not to lie within the purview of Title VII even though discrimination was found to have been proved. The possibility of quota relief is now being challenged in cases raising reverse discrimination issues. Eliminating such relief would considerably curtail the impact a finding of discrimination would have on restructuring the work force.

THE RELATIONSHIP BETWEEN TITLE VII AND AFFIRMATIVE ACTION

Two questions are currently before the Courts: (1) Does Title VII authorize quota relief? (A number of courts has held that it does not.)[117] (2) Are quotas, adopted voluntarily, pursuant to Executive Order violative of Title VII? In *United Steel Workers of America* v. *Weber*,[118] the Supreme Court held that "Title VII's prohibition... against racial discrimination does not condemn all private, voluntary, race-conscious affirmative action plans." The Court spoke solely in terms of racial discrimination, emphasizing that the legislative history of Title VII indicated that the law had been "triggered by a Nation's concern over centuries of racial injustice."[119] The government, in its brief, had conceded that quotas are not authorized by the Executive Order in the absence of substantial evidence of past discrimination. Despite the favorable outcome of *Weber*, therefore, it may be considerably more difficult for women than for members of racial minority groups to establish that they are entitled to affirmative action because of past discrimination by an employer, especially given Justice Powell's language in *Bakke*.

Other employment-related activities by grantees

Executive orders. Since Executive Order 11246, as amended by Executive Order 11375, which prohibits sex discrimination by employers who hold contracts with the federal government, has been held not to give a private right of action, the grantees' main

---

116. 585 F.2d 192 (6th Cir. 1978).

117. *See, e.g.,* Mitchell v. Mid-Continent Spring Co. of Kentucky, 587 F. 2d 841 (6th Cir. 1978).

118. 99 S.Ct. 2721, 2730 (1979).

119. Ibid., p. 2728.

concern has been to force the Department of Labor to adopt regulations requiring contractors to establish affirmative action goals and timetables. As a result of two lawsuits instituted by the League of Women Voters against the Secretary of Labor, proposed regulations requiring federal contractors to set goals and timetables for the hiring of female bricklayers, carpenters, painters, plasterers, and others in the construction industry were published in 1977 and finally promulgated in 1978.

The Center for Law and Social Policy is representing an organization called Women Employed in its efforts to intervene in an administrative proceeding initiated by the Departments of Treasury and Labor to force a Chicago Bank to meet its affirmative action obligations as a federal contractor pursuant to the Executive Order. The case raises the issue of whether back pay may be awarded to the affected class and whether Federal Depository Funds may be cut off.

Job-training programs. The Women's Rights Project of the Center for Law and Social Policy joined with other groups in bringing an administrative petition requesting the Labor Department to amend its regulations dealing with equal employment opportunity in all federally registered apprenticeship programs so as to require specific affirmative action for women. Interested women and women's organizations worked together with Department of Labor officials to draft the regulations that were promulgated in 1978. In light of reverse discrimination issues, the regulations carefully spell out a history of past discrimination against women.

Both the Women's Rights Project of the Center for Law and Social Policy and the Chicana Rights Project of MALDEF have successfully challenged plans drawn up under the Comprehensive Employment and Training Act (CETA) as inadequately meeting the needs of unemployed women.

Military. The WRP, League of Women Voters, and the Center for Law and Social Policy have all been engaged in litigation seeking to open opportunities for women in the military, a traditional route to employment for those of limited skills and opportunities.

EDUCATION

Little has as yet been accomplished via litigation toward achieving equal opportunity for women in education.

Title IX

The key statutory provisions for attacking sex discrimination in schools is Title IX of the Civil Rights Act of 1974 which states in pertinent part:

> No person in the United States shall, on the basis of sex, be excluded from participation in, be denied the benefits of, or be subjected to discrimination under any educational program or activity receiving federal financial assistance...

Although Title IX was passed in 1972, the regulations defining its contours were not issued until 1975 by the Department of Health, Education and Welfare. Unfortunately, no one to date has done much to enforce the Act.

Implementation by HEW. The Act provides for the administrative enforcement of its provisions, the sanction being the cut-off of federal funds. Because of a total lack of implementation by HEW—no federal funds had ever been cut off from any school for noncompliance with the antidiscriminatory provisions—the Center for Law and Social Policy, as counsel for Women's Equity Action League (WEAL), instituted a court proceeding challenging the nonenforcement of the federal laws prohibiting sex discrimination in the educational system. In December 1977, it obtained a court order in *Adams* v. *Califano*, directing HEW and the Department of Labor to institute enforcement proceedings. The Center continues to monitor the order. Since the second set of reports from HEW is overdue, the attorneys at the Center suspect that compliance pursuant to the order is well behind schedule and that a contempt order may have to be sought. Severe misgivings have been expressed about some of the Title IX regulations which are viewed as articulating a less favorable policy toward women than the Title VII regulations.[120] The Center is watching developments with regard to these guidelines.

120. On the other hand, the National Collegiate Athletic Association challenged the applicability of Title IX guidelines to intercollegiate athletics, and athletic scholarships. The Center intervened in support of the regulations. The district court dismissed

Private right of action. Because administrative enforcement of Title IX was so sadly lacking, an attempt was made, in which a number of the grantees joined, to bypass implementation by HEW by arguing that the person discriminated against has a right to institute a court proceeding because a private right of action can be implied under Title IX. Except for one case handled by the Women's Law Fund,[121] the lower courts had rejected the private right of action concept. In *Cannon v. University of Chicago*,[122] the Supreme Court held that Title IX created a private right of action for the victims of illegal discrimination, thus opening a vast new area for litigation, since Title IX touches virtually every aspect of life in educational institutions. The regulations deal with admissions, counseling, course offerings, housing, financial assistance, student employment, general university employment, health and insurance benefits for employees, health services for students, marital and parental status, and physical education and athletics.

Even if complainants other than HEW are given the power to enforce Title IX, it is questionable whether discriminatory employment practices by educational institutions are encompassed within the scope of the Act. A number of courts have held employment to be governed exclusively by Title VII.[123] The sorry record in overcoming discrimination in institutions of higher learning pursuant to Title VII was discussed above.

Vocational Education Act. Although a number of grantees, especially the WRP, have expressed an interest in mounting a campaign to challenge discrimination in vocational education, thus far no litigation has been initiated, even though the WRP has prepared a vocational education litigation kit. The explanation offered is the inability to find clients.

Constitutional challenges. A number of cases have challenged unequal opportunity in educational institutions on the basis of

the complaint for lack of standing, and an appeal is currently pending in the Tenth Circuit.

121. Piascik v. Cleveland Museum of Art, 426 F.Supp. 779 (N.D. Ohio 1976).

122. 99 S.Ct. 1946 (1979).

123. See, e.g., Romeo Community Schools v. HEW, 438 F.Supp. 1021 (E.D. Mich. 1976).

the Fourteenth Amendment. Sex-segregated schools and teams have been attacked on the ground that separate but equal treatment is unconstitutional. As was mentioned above, a lower court decision upholding sex-segregated schools in Philadelphia was affirmed without opinion by the Supreme Court in *Vorchheimer v. School District.*[124]

In *Yellow Springs Exempted Village School District Board of Education v. Ohio High School Athletic Association,* a Women's Law Fund case, a district judge held that a regulation of the State High School Athletic Association which prohibited girls from participating with boys in contact sports violated the due process clause of the Fourteenth Amendment. While acknowledging the state's legitimate interest in preventing injury to participants and in maximizing female athletic opportunities, the court found that such state interests and the challenged association rules were the product of a conclusive presumption that all girls are physically weaker and less proficient athletes than boys.[126] Because all women do not necessarily suffer similar disabilities, girls who so desire must be given an opportunity to demonstrate the invalidity of the presumption, and, if successful, be permitted to compete with boys in contact sports. Finally, the judge declared unconstitutional the regulations promulgated pursuant to Title IX authorizing separate but equal teams in contact sports. Other cases as well have successfully raised the issue of women being excluded from all boys teams on the basis of the equal protection clause, although some claims of discrimination have been rejected when there is a comparable female team or when the sport in which the woman seeks to engage is a contact, rather than noncontact sport.[127]

A suit by the Women's Law Fund alleging that the distribution of financial aid at the University of Minnesota, which was based upon the recipient's ability to repay, disadvantaged all but white males and, therefore, violated the Fourteenth Amendment, was settled favorably after four years of litigation.

124. *See* note 48.

125. 443 F.Supp. 753 (S.D. Ohio 1978).

126. *See* discussion of the due process argument on p. 33.

127. *See* Note, *Sex Discrimination in High School Athletics,* 47 UMKC Law Review, 109, 110–113 (1978).

OTHER AREAS OF LITIGATION

Health

The Women's Rights Project of the Center for Law and Social Policy has been particularly active in the health area. It has been engaged in litigation challenging regulations issued by HEW as not sufficiently protecting those participating in federal programs, or receiving health care with federal funding, from being involuntarily sterilized. The Center has also represented a number of women's organizations that intervened in a suit brought by the Pharmaceutical Manufacturers Association and the American College of Obstetricians and Gynecologists to challenge the authority of the FDA to require patient package inserts for estrogen-based drugs. The court denied the preliminary injunction sought by the plaintiffs, and the case is going forward on the merits.

Credit

The League of Women Voters has instituted an action pursuant to the Equal Credit Opportunity Act which prohibits creditors from discriminating on the basis of sex and marital status in any aspect of a credit transaction.

Property rights

The League of Women Voters, as amicus curiae, has been engaged in litigation challenging the constitutionality of the "head and master" provision in the Louisiana Civil Code which gives the husband absolute control over community property unless the parties expressly contract otherwise prior to marriage.

UNLITIGATED OR UNDERLITIGATED AREAS

Women as consumers

With the exception of the League's credit suit, very little litigation has yet been undertaken with regard to issues such as credit and mortgage lending. Furthermore, no systematic attack has yet been launched on discriminatory insurance practices, although some aspects of this problem have been touched upon in the pregnancy disability and pension plan cases. The Center for

Law and Social Policy and the Women's Law Fund have both expressed an interest in the insurance field.

Virtually no litigation activity by grantees has centered on criminal law. The Women's Law Fund would like to challenge the denial of equal educational opportunities to women incarcerated in state penal institutions.

Occupational and Safety Health Act

A number of the grantees fear that the Occupational Safety and Health Act (OSHA) will be used as a pretext for discrimination, operating in the same way as the protectionist laws did prior to their successful challenge under Title VII. Employers have already begun to remove female workers from certain jobs for their "own good," while continuing to allow male employees to work in these environments without making any attempt to ascertain the effect this may have on their fertility or future offspring. Thus far, the grantees are monitoring the work of the administrative bodies charged with responsibility in this area, and are consulting with various concerned groups. No litigative strategy has, as yet, emerged, and there does not seem to be a clear consensus on the policy the women's groups should adopt. Should they protest regulations restricting female work as discriminatory to women since they interfere with a woman's right to work, and to choose for herself whether to risk harm? Or should they seek to include males within the scope of the regulations?

Women and the family

Since almost all of the grantees' activity has centered on the federal courts, very little of the litigative effort has been spent on questions that lie within the exclusive competence of the states, such as the laws governing marriage and divorce, children, property rights, and inheritance.

Evaluating the Litigative Effort

SHORTCOMINGS

Although many substantive gains have been achieved through the litigation process, the results discussed previously indicate an unwillingness on the part of the courts to accommodate the law to the tremendous changes that have taken place in the structure of work and family life. It is also apparent that there are still large groups of women on whose lives the litigation effort has not yet had much of an impact.

The uncooperative attitudes of the courts

In part, the Supreme Court's reluctance to extend the full protection of the equal protection clause to women may be attributable to a feeling that the legislature rather than the judiciary is the appropriate body for policy making of such a fundamental nature, especially given the historical context in which the Fourteenth Amendment was adopted. The language of some of the justices, the results in other courts, and in Title VII cases where Congress has spoken, however, are suggestive of more than deference to the legislative branch. Many of the judges do not yet seem to understand how the present system discriminates against women. Not only have the courts drawn back when a favorable decision for women would mean a fundamental change in the way business is done in the United States, but there are indications that the federal courts are reacting more unfavorably now than they did when the litigation effort first began. The courts' insistence on higher standards of proof of discrimination, and their unwillingness to grant certain kinds of effective relief even when discrimination has been proven are illustrative. The reverse discrimination issue and growing employer intransigence such as that manifested by *Sears Roebuck's* recently instituted suit against the government claiming an inability to comply with the antidiscrimination laws, are further indications that a backlash has developed in reaction to the substantive gains that have been achieved.[128]

128. Sears, Roebuck and Co. v. Attorney General, 47 V.S.L.W. 2734 (1979).

The failure to reach certain groups

Sex-segregated employees and blue-collar workers. For the most part, the litigation effort to date has not been able to achieve substantial gains for the great majority of women who work in sex-segregated jobs. Title VII litigation has enabled some women to move into nontraditional work, but the statistics indicate that a very small percentage of the female work force has been able to make such a move to date. As the earnings gap between male and female wages reflects, the litigation effort has not been able to reach the wage structure for traditional female work. No way has as yet been found to deal with the issue of equal pay for comparable work. Blue-collar women, who are probably the most tradition minded, and the most subject to dominance by men, have barely been touched by the litigation effort. The litigators have not made contact with the unions, who, with the notable exception of the International Union of Electrical Workers, which instituted the *Gilbert* case and many other actions challenging sex discrimination, have done virtually nothing for their female members. The unions are not supporting women who are being disproportionately laid off when men are being laid off, too, and have hardly begun to bargain with employers on issues specific to women. Despite the large and growing number of women who belong to unions, women are almost nonexistent in the governing hierarchies.

Minority women. Nobody is really speaking on behalf of the black working woman at this time. Since traditionally she could often get a job when the black male could not, the problem is not one of getting her into the work force but of improving her condition there, which is at the very bottom of the wage structure. Part of the difficulty in doing so is the same as with all women who work in the lower echelon sex-segregated job, but, in addition, the black woman is viewed as a threat to the black man. Since a black woman counts double in an employer's minority worker statistics, it is feared that black women may seem more desirable than black men. Consequently, organized black groups do not seem to be pushing their women.

This particular problem does not seem to exist in respect to the Chicana woman who, because of a completely different cultural past, was never part of the work force at all. Her difficulty lies in leaving the house in order to work. Once she manages this, her earnings are recognized as being good for the family. The attorneys at MALDEF did not perceive a conflict between the demands of the women and the demands of the men, at least at this time.

Drawbacks inherent in the litigative process
Finally, it must be remembered that litigation is slow and expensive, and hard on the willing litigant. A legislative strategy can be faster, and sometimes cheaper, and may be easier to package because there is no need to raise the issue in the context of a client with standing. Favorable legislation constitutes an empty promise unless it is enforced, however, and the litigation effort on behalf of women's rights was organized precisely because the legislative gains of the 1960s did not translate into benefits for women.

IMPORTANCE OF THE LITIGATION EFFORT
The effort by the litigating groups, and especially the grantees, has been extremely important, even though the initially targeted objectives have not been completely achieved and despite the ensuing backlash.

Litigation for implementation
Governmental enforcement. In the absence of a litigation effort, the implementation of the existing statutes and executive orders prohibiting sex discrimination would have been far worse. Even though Title VII and IX vest prime responsibility for enforcement in the administrative agencies, rather than in the private litigant, women have not been able to rely on the agencies to discharge their statutory obligations. The EEOC, charged with the implementation of Title VII, has permitted such an enormous backlog[129] to accumulate that it has abandoned systemic programs and class action investigations while it catches up.[130] The record with

129. Tamar, *On and Off the Record*, National Law Journal, August 7, 1978, p. 39. "The EEOC currently has an inventory of more than 100,000 complaints that have been filed but not settled—some of them several years old."

130. House Labor Subcommittee on Employment Opportunities (statement of Eleanor

regard to Title IX has been even worse. At least the EEOC has issued regulations that are favorable to women. Not only are the regulations issued pursuant to Title IX considerably less helpful, but there has been a total failure to implement Title IX to date. When implementation begins it will be due to the litigative effort: (1) either because of compliance with the order obtained by the Center for Law and Social Policy directing the Secretary of HEW to undertake enforcement procedures, and/or (2) because the Supreme Court has implied a private right of action under Title IX.[131] Regulations issued pursuant to the executive orders, which added goals for women, did so because of pressure from the women's groups, including the grantees.[132]

Enforcement by the private bar. Would equivalent substantive gains have been achieved in the absence of a litigative effort by groups enjoying philanthrophic support? Definitely not. Virtually all of the doctrinal development of the seminal issues of sex-based discrimination has been achhieved through the efforts of the not-for-profit sector of the bar, and especially through groups funded by foundations. Constitutional litigation requires a persistence of effort, resources, and management beyond the capabilities of the private litigant.[133] Even though the successful litigant in a Title VII action may be awarded attorneys' fees and costs, the outlay required for discovery and experts while the litigation is in progress, potentially a period of many years, makes most Title VII litigation financially unfeasible for all but large firms, especially now that defendants are less prone to settle quickly.

A recent survey by the New York Law Journal of all women law firms (nineteen were located) suggests that many of them have had to engage in general practice, primarily domestic relations work, in order to be able to afford taking cases involving women's rights, which is what they had really wanted to do, but which is obviously not profitable.

Holmes Norton, Chair, EEOC, at oversight hearings), reported at 99 L.R.R. 289 (December 11, 1978).

131. See p. 65.

132. See p. 61.

133. See C. Vose, *Constitutional Change* (1972); R. Kluger, *Simple Justice* (1976).

The work done by some of the grantees in monitoring the performance of government agencies, both in rule making and enforcement, could not be afforded by the women's groups who are the clients, if they had to pay prevailing legal rates.

Litigation as a component of political action

Gilbert v. *General Electric Co.*[134] is instructive on both the limitations and importance of the litigative effort. If one looks only at the result in the case itself, which reversed the favorable determinations on pregnancy disability that had been obtained in the lower courts, *Gilbert* probably represents the single greatest defeat suffered by the litigators. On the other hand, until *Gilbert*, many female employees and labor unions were completely oblivious of the pregnancy disability issue despite favorable results, and were not asking or bargaining for disability coverage. It was only the high visibility of the Supreme Court's decision that turned *Gilbert* into the catalyst needed to bring into being a coalition spearheaded by the ACLU, which convinced Congress to amend Title VII to bring pregnancy discrimination within its purview. The new amendment, besides reversing *Gilbert* so that pregnancy may not be excluded from disability plans, also reverses that portion of *Satty* which had permitted employers to deny employees the use of accumulated sick leave for maternity purposes, and prohibits forced leaves of pregnant workers prior to actual disability. It is unlikely that the Congress, which added sex discrimination to Title VII in 1964 as an afterthought, would have included pregnancy disability at that time. It is only because the issue worked its way slowly into public consciousness through the EEOC regulations, the commentary on the lower court decisions, and the outraged reaction to the Supreme Court's opinion that a climate was prepared in which Congress was willing to act because it could now understand how much this issue meant to women. Thus, *Gilbert*, far from being a defeat, should be viewed as a triumph, because the legislative effort it triggered led to an enormous substantive gain for pregnant employees which will restructure some of the basic working relationships for women. The lesson to be drawn from *Gilbert* and its aftermath is clear. Litigation is a marvelous tool,

134. *See* pp. 29, 40–42.

but it must be used in conjunction with the political process, particularly now, when the courts are obviously looking to Congress to make the changes that will affect the economic position of women in our society.

Litigation as a weapon

There seems to be a consensus that the threat of lawsuits has caused women to be taken more seriously. Until the litigation effort began, the women's rights movement was a topic for conversation, not action, even after Title VII and the Equal Pay Act had been passed.

Even though compliance is far from exemplary now and there has been no real statistical change, the litigation effort has given at least some women an opportunity to prove their competence in jobs which they would not previously have held.[135] Even the unsuccessful lawsuit may create a positive ripple effect, because one of the messages that gets conveyed is the enormous cost to the defendant in time and money, particularly since in Title VII actions the prevailing defendant will not ordinarily be able to recover attorneys' fees. Thus, despite the terrible results in cases involving higher education, WEAL reports that the percentage of women in all levels of academia is increasing.

Litigation and consciousness raising

It is almost impossible to pick up a newspaper or magazine, or to turn on the radio or television without coming across some reference to the changing role of women. The frequency with which the litigation effort is given some credit highlights not only its impact but its newsworthiness. Supreme Court cases dealing with sex-based discrimination make the front page; magazines sold in supermarkets contain articles reporting on the latest litigation efforts; new publications, geared specifically to the working woman, are particularly informative about legal rights and gains.

Each of the grantees has been the subject of numerous newspaper stories, and the attorneys are frequently asked for their comments when a significant decision involving women is issued by a court. The grantees have also spent a sizeable

135. See pp. 10-12.

portion of their time on educational programs, ranging from training law students and speaking at legal seminars to participating in events involving the general public. Thus, the significance of the grantee's work is disseminated well beyond the courtroom and may play a significant role in eliminating stereotyped notions about women, and in raising the expectations of women as to what they can choose to accomplish with their lives. Many of the grantees, as well as other foundation-supported litigating groups, are involved in clinical programs at law schools. These serve a dual function: they give the litigators some sorely needed assistance, while at the same time sensitizing the students and equipping them with the necessary skills to be effective advocates of women's rights once they have graduated.

Making the Litigation Effort More Effective

IMPROVING THE CASE SELECTION PROCESS

With a few exceptions, the advocacy efforts on behalf of women's rights has proceeded on an ad hoc basis. Litigators have chosen their clients from among the persons who walked through the office door; rarely have they identified problems, established priorities, and then followed through with a search for an appropriate client. Although many of the litigators complain about the difficulty of finding plaintiffs, the inability to find a suitable case can become a self-fulfilling prophecy. If planning is ignored because it is seen as futile, contacts are neglected with the very groups whose involvement may produce good case material, such as grass roots organizations, the media, local attorneys, university communities, and other organized groups and networks. While litigation cannot be controlled completely—there will always be some litigants with private counsel, or even pro se claimants, indifferent to larger strategic concerns—the unachievability of total control does not negate all benefits that would accrue from identifying and implementing litigative priorities. With the Supreme Court's recent decision in *In re Primus*[136] which recognizes a First Amendment right on the part of public interest organizations such as the ACLU to render advice to prospective clients about the feasibility of litigation, many of the ethical concerns about solicitation have been alleviated.

Strategic concerns
Since many of the litigators feel that the litigation effort has lost momentum this would seem an appropriate time to target new issues and goals. Furthermore, changes have occurred in our economy and work force that may require a new response.[137]

Identifying the appropriate approach. The litigators need to devise new strategies in terms of their progress to date:

Are appropriate plaintiffs being used? In part, the courts' lack of sympathy to claims of sex discrimination may be due to a failure to grasp the consequences. The effects of racial discrimination are far more obvious: judges can see ghettos, race riots, and segregated schools. Confronted with a claim of sex discrimination , the jurists seem to think of the comfortable lives of the middle-class women whom they know best, such as their own wives and daughters. Because employment discrimination actions rarely reach the woman at the bottom of the employment structure, judges are perhaps insufficiently aware of the millions of women who work not by choice, but out of necessity, to support themselves and their families. An effort should be made to structure litigation with these women as plaintiffs in order to bring them and their problems to the attention of the courts, as for instance, through cases involving issues of consumer or family or property law.

New objectives have to be identified and sought through litigation. For instance, given the increased cost and difficulties of proof in Title VII actions, the hope of furthering the doctrinal development of employment discrimination law may have to be abandoned, at least temporarily, in favor of other objectives.

136. 98 S.Ct. 1893 (1978).

137. See Part II.

Perhaps a coordinated multi-jurisdiction campaign should be instituted with regard to particular kinds of nontraditional jobs for women. Or perhaps the litigators should try to generate some winning momentum by concentrating on suits against employers who may even now be particularly vulnerable to settlements, because they have the most to lose if they fall out of favor with women, such as cosmetic firms, women's wear manufacturers, or supermarkets. Other areas in which litigation has proceeded have to be reassessed to determine whether the initial objective still makes sense.

Are there *new areas of the law* that could be targeted for doctrinal development, such as the laws dealing with insurance, credit, and mortgages that affect women as consumers?

Are there stronger strategies that could be developed with regard to *unsuccessful areas*, such as discrimination in higher education? A greater organizational effort to locate good plaintiffs, coupled with a careful choice of the jurisdiction in which to proceed, might yield better results.

Priorities have to be assigned for issue development. For instance, if a private right of action is implied under Title IX, a detailed strategy must be developed in order to ensure the raising of some of the more sensitive issues, such as pushing females into different curricula than males, rather than the more obvious, but less detrimental practices, such as discrimination on athletic teams.

Negative effects have to be anticipated in order to prepare an appropriate defensive strategy. For instance, if accelerated technological change resulting in the loss of women's jobs is the concomitant of affirmative action in behalf of women,[138] the litigators must face up to the exceedingly difficult issue of whether and how technological change should be resisted or tempered, perhaps through provisions in consent decrees or collective bargaining agreements.[139] A related problem is the proper strategic defense against lay-offs that impact disproportionately on women because they were hired last. As was

138. See p. 16.

139. Cf. Burke & Chase, *Resolving the Seniority Minority Layoffs Conflict: An Employer-Targeted Approach*, 13 Harvard Civil Rights-Civil Liberties Law Review 81 (1978). The proposal would prevent employer from passing on burden of hiring minority employees to majority employees by laying them off.

discussed above, the litigators though sensitive to the potential effects of OSHA have not yet decided on an appropriate course of action.

Numerous other factors need to be considered in case selection, such as the desirability of raising the same issue simultaneously in a number of different jurisdictions, selecting the most favorable jurisdictions for the issue in question, estimating the technical assistance that will be required, assessing the support that can be rallied for the issue, selecting back-up cases in order to consolidate gains or to limit losses.

Implementation. When the litigative effort began, the grantees' prime objective was to select cases suitable for the doctrinal development of key concepts such as equal protection, disparate impact, the bfoq defense, etc. For the moment, however, the federal courts have indicated an unwillingness to break new ground. Instead of risking further inhospitable reactions, this may be the time to think about consolidating gains.

Because the litigators put their limited resources into making new law, they were never able to follow through on their successes. For instance, after the Women's Law Fund won *Cleveland Board of Education* v. *LaFleur*,[140] the case which invalidated the mandatory pregnancy leave policy of the defendant as violative of the due process clause, it was offered the opportunity to handle hundreds of similar cases. Had it accepted these requests for representation, it would not have been able to go forward with any new litigation, but it might have put the due process argument on a stronger footing, and raised the consciousness of the community about the impact of pregnancy on a working woman's life. Now that new litigation is less desirable, the benefits of consolidating prior victories should be reassessed. Part of the explanation for the lack of statistical change in the earnings of women may be due to failures in implementing past successes. Even though the issue of law is clear, the issues of fact or the procedural complexities may still make the case too expensive or too difficult for the private bar to handle, so that many of the follow-up cases are probably abandoned.

Obviously, attorneys of the caliber who have been working for

140. See note 64, p. 33.

the grantees would not want to relinquish all innovative litigation. At this time, however, they might be able to devote some of their time to garden variety follow-up cases, particularly if they had more paralegal assistance to whom routinized procedures could be entrusted. The litigators should also explore cooperative implementation efforts with some of the new legal clinics that are beginning to spring up in response to *Bates* v. *State Bar of Arizona*.[141]

Selecting the appropriate court. In light of recent unfavorable developments in the federal courts, the time may have come to begin a litigative effort in the state courts, some of which have issued opinions far more beneficial than decisions on comparable issues in federal jurisdictions. Furthermore, in those states which have enacted ERAs, a litigative effort could be mounted that could not be paralleled in the federal courts; and even in non-ERA states issues could be litigated that do not lie within the competence of the federal courts, such as questions involving the family, property, and inheritance. Of course, some states do not have favorable laws at all, and litigators in those states would still have to resort to the federal forum.

It would not be wise to abandon the national litigative effort completely. Such a move would be viewed as leaving the field to the enemy and would result in a tremendous loss of face, particularly since the federal courts are generally seen as more prestigious. Furthermore, the ability to pressure Congress to pass effective legislation would be lessened considerably if no effort is made to implement the statutes that have been enacted. The proper role of women in our society is a national question that has to be articulated in a national forum, but the state courts may be a valuable, virtually untouched resource at this time.

Grass roots organization

Although a number of the grantees have represented women's organizations in litigation, the litigative effort has not been integrated with grass-roots reform efforts. The grantees, with the

141. 433 U.S. 350 (1977). (This held that truthful advertising of routine legal services is protected by the First and Fourteenth Amendments.)

exception of MALDEF, and to a lesser degree Public Advocates, are isolated from their constituencies. There is an obvious lack of connection between the feminist movement and the litigation effort. While a good deal of this may be due to a lack of organization by women's groups rather than any fault on the part of the litigators, the consequences of this failure for the litigative efforts are severe.

Case selection. The inability to find clients to litigate in the vocational education field is certainly attributable to the lack of ties the grantees have to women with children studying vocational education. Until the litigators establish channels of communication with other networks of women, the litigation effort will continue to serve primarily as a vehicle for achieving gains for upper- and middle-class women, the only groups that will search out an attorney when a problem arises.

Support for the litigant. Virtually every litigator commented spontaneously on the tremendous toll litigation imposes on the litigant, a toll which makes the litigators' task much harder. The harassment and scapegoating to which the litigant is subject, particularly if she is still working for the named defendant, often form the basis for additional claims of discrimination. The litigators concede that many of their clients are persons who have always been at odds with the rest of the world; since society frowns on aggressive women, "nice" women who are discriminated against get themselves a new job. Litigation exacerbates all of the claimants' problems. Most of the litigators estimate that fully 50 per cent of their clients suffer from some form of legal psychosis. Unlike the racial minority litigant who has a community to fall back on, the victim in a sex discrimination case often has only her attorney to whom to turn. The litigators feel themselves ill-equipped to deal with these demands for support, which in addition, can consume a great deal of their time. If litigants emerged from organized groups of women, they would undoubtedly feel less anxious to begin with, and would also be able to secure far more reassurance than a busy litigator is able to give. Problems in obtaining plaintiffs and keeping plaintiffs would thereby be lessened.

Support for the litigation. Finally, in a much larger sense, organization may be the key to victory in the courts. History shows that major social change is not endorsed by the judiciary until a certain level of support for the new social movement has been generated outside the courtroom. Unless more support is rallied for the objectives of the women's rights movement at local political levels, it is unlikely that the attitude of the federal judiciary will undergo a drastic change. A number of interviewees suggested a correlation between the increasing hostility of the courts and the difficulties encountered in passing the ERA. If judges reflect social attitudes, then the most effective way to change their outlook is to organize public support for the issues that they will encounter. Consequently, more attention should be paid to refuting the concerns of those who oppose the ERA, whose genuine fears about what will happen are undoubtedly shared by the courts.

Geographical organization

If the grantees had to chart the location of the active litigators on behalf of women's rights, most of them would come up with a pictorial representation resembling the cartoon map Saul Steinberg drew of the United States as a *New Yorker* cover: New York and Washington would appear on the map and the rest of the country would barely be acknowledged until one arrived in California.[142] On the other hand, the cases that the litigators are handling are scattered all over the United States. What are the drawbacks of this sytem, and can any improvements be made at this time?

Certainly, the grantees have the capacity to handle appellate work effectively regardless of where the appellate court is located. But when these groups undertake a case *ab initio*, problems emerge. A protracted trial far from the home office is hard on the litigator, puts considerable strain on the resources of the group back home, and causes a lot of time to be wasted on transportation. A local group may be able to establish closer ties with the local governmental agencies concerned, have easier

---

142. This is not intended as a slur against the Women's Law Fund of Cleveland, but solely to point out that it is somewhat separate from the New York-Washington-California axis.

(and cheaper) access to local experts, and have friendlier relations with local judges and juries. Working effectively with local cooperating attorneys can alleviate some of these problems, provided that such groups exist, and provided they have been integrated into the litigation effort.

With the increased number of women law school graduates, many of whom may have had some exposure to sex discrimination law in school, this may be an appropriate time for a concerted effort to identify and recruit a network of cooperating attorneys. Encouraging a local litigation effort might achieve some of the objectives sought via grass roots organization, since local litigators in smaller communities may be able to achieve enough of an identity so that local women with grievances will turn to them for information and advice.[143] Furthermore, the point of view outside New York, Washington, and California may be somewhat different and needs to be incorporated into long-range planning. To some extent, the affiliates of national organizations like the ACLU and the League of Women Voters serve the same function, but not all of these affiliates have established ties with women's groups nor the expertise to litigate effectively.

Alliances with other groups

With some exceptions, the litigators have done little to form coalitions for litigation with groups outside the women's rights area, although they have cooperated effectively in administrative and legislative efforts. One way to avoid a double standard in sex and race cases is to structure a case so as to raise both claims together. Little contact has been achieved with other groups, which on certain issues may have interests in common with women, such as organized labor, or at least women in organized labor. Alliances with consumer groups and environmental groups (e.g., OSHA) should certainly be investigated. The need for greater communication with other organized groups should be considered when setting up workshops, conferences, and strategy sessions.

---

143. The Women's Law Fund reported over 200 general referral and information phone calls in each six month period augmented by an average of 100 calls for assistance from the bar.

Interdisciplinary input

Most of the litigators are unaware of the work being done by social scientists at universities in the area of women's rights. This ignorance hampers their ability to comprehend the past, to assess the consequences of their work, and to plan for the future. Long-range planning could be more responsive if the litigators were briefed on trends that will affect women's lives such as demographic changes, shifts in employment patterns, technological change, etc. Is there, for instance, any point in attacking sex-segregated educational institutions, if the expected decline in the number of students means that the school system will soon not be able to afford two schools?

IMPROVING THE CAPACITY TO LITIGATE

It is a tribute to the competence and devotion of the grantees that they have managed to service their clients so well. In doing so, they have been forced to operate as investigators, fund-raisers, speechwriters, educators, public relations experts, psychiatrists, and data analysts, to name only a few of their tasks. Freeing the litigators from some of these jobs would enable them to utilize their expertise more effectively. Two suggestions are offered: (1) to provide the grantee with additional personnel and to relieve them of some of their monitoring work, and (2) a much more far-reaching solution that would require the creation of a new centralized back-up center. Both proposals would give the attorneys more of an of an opportunity to concentrate on litigation.

The need for paralegal personnel and monitoring assistance

Numerous functions currently performed by the attorneys could more profitably be handled by paralegals. For instance, why should a highly trained attorney be spending her time reading computer printouts to see whether a large employer is abiding by the terms of a consent decree? Numerous other activities centering on the investigative, discovery, and compliance phases of litigation could also be handled profitably by paraprofessionals as is now done in large law firms. Law students working for the grantees as part of a clinical program cannot be used for this kind of work because it is too devoid of educational value to warrant course credit.

Any consent decree or judgment ordering class relief is likely to be so complicated as to require a large expenditure of time to ensure that its provisions are really being followed. For instance, the WRP has had problems monitoring the results in its cases against the New York restaurants who refused to hire waitresses, because each of the twelve cases terminated with a somewhat different agreement with somewhat different deadlines and terms. The Women's Law Fund spends valuable time checking out the semi-annual reports with which it is furnished pursuant to the consent decree it obtained in the policewomen cases it handled. Monitoring will become even more of a problem if the litigation effort expands and becomes more successful, yet effective monitoring is essential if viable victories rather than paper gains are to be achieved.

Furnishing the grantees with paralegal personnel might lessen this problem. Another possible solution might be to farm out monitoring to some other group. There is no reason why some of the women's groups could not undertake this type of activity, under the supervision of an attorney, so as to free the grantees for other work; or there could be a central organization, one of whose functions would be to provide monitoring services.

The need for a centralized back-up center

Two major and very different problems exist with respect to the litigation effort: (1) the factual proof of discrimination has become increasingly technical and expensive, and (2) in order to make litigation efforts more effective, coordination efforts need to be improved. The establishment of a centralized back-up center under foundation auspices to which the grantees, and other litigating groups, would have access could ameliorate both of these problems.

Since so much of current litigation depends on statistics and other expert proof, a back-up center with computer capabilities, staffed by a corps of experts such as statisticians, programmers, juristic psychologists, and economists, perhaps in conjunction with a university program, could serve a number of functions directly related to litigation. It could (1) provide expert input at the planning stage of litigation, (2) supply experts to actually testify at trial, (3) evaluate defense experts and/or independent experts selected by the grantees, (4) develop standard programs for use in more than one lawsuit, (5) store computerized data, and (6) design programs for monitoring decrees and judgments.

Such a center could also play an important role in coordinating the litigation effort. To be most effective, strategic planning needs the imput of local organizations, networks, and other disciplines, and then has to be integrated with the agenda of the litigating groups and brought to the attention of the media. This requires a coordinating effort that has always proved difficult because of the decentralized nature of the litigation effort in behalf of women's rights. While decentralization undoubtedly results in a healthy diversity of approach, it may also lead to some inefficiency and duplication of effort, primarily in the obtaining and dissemination of information. Making a particular grantee the coordinator for a particular issue or area of the law is unwieldy when one is talking about autonomous organizations, who are primarily engaged in a national litigation effort, in a country the size of the United States. Assigning clearinghouse functions in a particular area to a grantee also has drawbacks. The clearinghouse function is separated from the coordination effort; there are too many clearinghouses that overlap while at the same time there are gaps; the litigators are often too busy to deal with inquiries about the materials in the clearinghouse or how to use them; and the grantees do not have the facilities for the systematic collection, classification, and dissemination of information.

A national back-up center could provide the coordination clearinghouse functions that would enhance the grantees' ability to perform more effectively. It could (1) organize strategy conferences, (2) provide research materials, (3) operate as a clearinghouse, and (4) develop an ongoing relationship with the media. These functions would interrelate with the litigation functions described above. For instance, the possibility of developing standardized programs might enhance the attractiveness of bringing certain kinds of cases simultaneously in a number of jurisdictions; the data collected for a strategy conference might be usable in connection with a case; the material prepared for a case could be worked up for the media. The litigators would be relieved of technical and administrative burdens so that they could devote their energies to strategic concerns and the creative development of the law.

Conclusion

It is impossible to give an exact answer to the question of what the impact of litigation on women's rights has been. In the first place, it is probably too soon to know whether there has been a transformation in the role of women in our society. The *Wall Street Journal* concluded a series of articles on men and women with a quotation from a professor affiliated with Harvard University:[144]

> The question is to what extent are we really witnessing real social change, or just fads in which only a small percentage are involved... I wonder if people studying our era fifty years from now will really accept the claim that this is a turning point.

Determining the effect of litigation in causing the changes that no one is quite sure have occurred is even more difficult. To the extent that change has taken place, however, it seems clear that litigation, and the publicity about litigation, have played a part.

Although the courts have not yet taken any giant steps to restructure our society because of the changing role of women, a foundation has been laid on which to build in the future. Although the early momentum in the federal courts has slackened, it is the conclusion of this report that the litigative effort must go forward, even though there may be losses for a time. Litigation alone, no matter how effectively pursued, cannot end sex discrimination, but litigation in conjunction with other lines of attack is an important tool in bringing about change.

144. *Wall Street Journal*, Nov. 30, 1977, B4, Col. 6.

PERSONS INTERVIEWED

GRANTEES
ACLU Women's Rights Project
  Ruth Bader Ginsburg
  Kathleen W. Peratis
  Susan Ross
  Margaret M. Young
  Pat Beyea

Center for Law and Social Policy,
Women's Rights Project
  Marcia D. Greenberger
  Margaret A. Kohn

League of Women Voters
  Katherine A. Mazzaferri

MALDEF Chicana Rights Project
  Vilma Martinez
  Patricia M. Vasquez
  Linda Hanten

NAACP Legal Defense Fund, Inc.
  Jean Fairfax
  Elaine Jones
  Phyllis McClure

Public Advocates, Inc.
  Robert Gnaizda

Women's Law Fund
  Jane M. Picker
  Barbara K. Besser
  Charles E. Guerrier

OTHERS

Marge Albert, Organizer,
  Distributive Workers of America,
  District No. 65; National Executive
  Board of CLUW (Coalition of
  Labor Union Women)

Rhonda Copelon, Esq.,
  Center for Constitutional Rights,
  New York, N.Y.

Mary Dunlop, Esq.,
  Equal Rights Advocates,
  San Francisco, Calif.

Cynthia Epstein, Co-Director,
  Program for Sex Roles in Social
  Change, Columbia University;
  Professor of Sociology, Queens
  College

Eli Ginzberg,
  A Barton Hepburn Professor of
  Economics; Director, Conservation
  of Human Resources, Columbia
  University

Carol S. Greenwald,
  Research Associate, Radcliffe
  Institute for Independent Study,
  Cambridge, Mass.

Beverly Gross, Esq.,
  General Counsel, American
  Federation of State, County
  and Municipal Employees,
  District No. 37.

Gwyn Hall,
  New York Telephone Co.,
  Department of Urban Affairs

Sharon Johnson,
  Unsuccessful plaintiff in Title VII
  suit charging sex discrimination
  in institution of higher learning

Hon. Roberta Karmel, Commissioner,
  Securities and Exchange
  Commission

Carol Lefcourt, Esq.,
  Partner in now disbanded all
  women law firm of Lefcourt,
  Kraft and Arber

Marilyn Levy,
  Rockefeller Brothers Fund

Judith Lichtman, Esq.,
  Women's Legal Defense Fund

Mary Murfree,
  Doctoral candidate, Center for
  Social Sciences, Columbia
  University

Carol Parr, Executive Director,
  WEAL Fund, Washington, D.C.

Suzanne Paul, Cofounder WOW
  (Women Office Workers)

Harriet Raab, Esq., Employment
  Rights Project, Columbia
  University School of Law

Sadie Robarts,
  London barrister studying women's
  rights movement in United States

Esther Schachter, Esq.

Catherine Schrier,
  Education Department, American
  Federation of State, County
  and Municipal Employees,
  District No. 37

Phyllis Segal, Esq.,
  General Counsel, NOW Legal
  Defense and Education Fund

Leonard Silk, Economic Editor,
  The New York Times

Robert Young,
  New York Telephone Co.,
  Department of Urban Affairs

QUESTIONNAIRE SENT TO GRANTEES PRIOR TO INTERVIEWS AS BASIS FOR DISCUSSION

1. Do your clients come to you directly, through referrals, or otherwise?

2. What criteria do you use for case selection?

3. What do you consider your greatest victory to date? Why?

4. What do you consider your greatest defeat? Why?

5. To what extent has litigation resolved the issues you were seeking to raise, or has further monitoring and enforcement been essential?

6. Are there issues which you feel no longer need to be litigated at all, or which can now be handled by private sector attorneys?

7. Are your legal priorities the same now as when you first started litigating? If they are not, what has caused you to change your initial strategy?

8. Are there any as yet unlitigated issues which you think will become ripe for litigation in the near future?

9. On what groups of women has your litigation had the greatest impact in terms of, e.g., occupation, economic class, minorities, age?

10. To what extent have you been used as a resource center in your community when an issue of women's rights is in the news? (I'll want to see your press clippings.)

11. To what extent do other groups in the country solicit your aid? (I'd be interested in letters asking for your help and your replies.)

12. To what extent do you cooperate with other groups active in the women's rights field?

13. Do you feel that there has been any duplication of effort which could be avoided by greater cooperation between groups?

14. What do you view as the most significant changes which have taken place since you first started litigating?

15. What approaches other than litigation should be utilized in achieving your goals?

16. Do you feel that a greater litigation effort on the state, rather than the federal level would be desirable?

In order that we can discuss these questions in some detail, I would appreciate your sending me as soon as possible:

1. With regard to completed litigation, citations to all reported opinions, or a copy of the opinion if it is not reported.

2. A docket of all pending litigation with a brief summary of the issues in the case and its present status.

3. A short statement about future litigation that you are presently considering.

Some Current Cases

A number of cases raising issues of significance for the women's rights movement are currently pending before the Supreme Court. The Court will have an opportunity to clarify its somewhat ambivalent attitude about a woman's right to an abortion in a series of four cases challenging the Hyde Amendment, which restricts the use of Medicaid funds for reimbursing the cost of therapeutic abortion. In one of these cases, *Harris v. McCrae*, No. 79-1268 (to be argued April 21, 1980), the judge below held that Congress violated the Due Process Clause when it authorized reimbursement only "where the life of the mother would be endangered if the fetus were carried to term" instead of using the "medically necessary" standard otherwise employed for services covered by Medicaid. On April 28, 1980, the Supreme Court granted certiorari in a case challenging the constitutionality of Louisiana's "head and master" provision which has been repealed since instigation of the lititgation.

On April 22, 1980, in *Wengler v. Druggist's Mutual Inc.*, 48L.W. 4459 (1980), the Supreme Court held that a Missouri statute that authorizes workers' compensation death benefits for the spouse of a female worker without regard to dependency, but conditions similar benefits for the spouse of a female worker upon proof of dependency or mental or physical incapacity resulted in a denial of equal protection. The Court relied primarily on the precedents established in the Social Security Acts cases brought by the Women's Rights Project (WRP) of the American Civil Liberties Union, but again declined to make sex a suspect classification as it had been urged to do by the WRP in its amicus curiae brief.

Important developments have taken place at other than the Supreme Court level. The WRP was successful at the District court level in *Peters v. Wayne State University*, the Title VII action challenging the pension and annuity plans offered by the Teachers Insurance Annuity Association and College Retirement Fund. In response to *Peters*, the *EEOC v. Colby* case discussed in the text, and a third case, *Spirt v. Teachers Insurance and Annuity Association* which also found some discrimination under Title VII in giving female workers smaller pension payments than men, TIAA-CREF has announced that it is seeking state insurance department approvals of a "unisex" mortality table to be used in determining benefits. This voluntary change would only apply to benefits resulting from premiums paid after the new tables are adopted. Litigation continues as to how to fashion a remedy for the past violations.

The Army, in response to pressure by the WRP, has abandoned its prior practice of using disparate enlistment criteria for men and women, which required superior qualifications for females. Litigation has been instituted on behalf of women who underwent sterilization when threatened with a loss of their jobs because chemicals or processes, allegedly dangerous to the fetus or potential fetus, are being used in the work place. Men are never excluded on these grounds despite evidence that their health is also affected adversely. The Equal Employment Opportunity Commission has issued interim guidelines for determining when an action constitutes unlawful sexual harassment in violation of Title VII.

MARGARET A. BERGER

MAY 1, 1980